AMERICA'S ARK

THE ONLY SAFE PLACE FOR AMERICANS TODAY

Don Schwarz

PRESS

Foreword

America's Ark

America's Ark is the book of the hour for the Christians in America. Pastor Don has taken an important warning from the Prophet Ezekiel and made it totally relevant to today. He shows how what happened to ancient Israel, when it turned from God, is now happening to America.

The book gives an excellent brief yet sweeping view of American history and how society was anchored in biblical principles. He then shows how this is all now washed away and replaced by rebellion against God. America now has no foundation. The problems facing America are beyond economic, social, or political. *America's Ark* shows the problem is that the biblical foundation has been washed away.

When a nation turns from the Bible, God then sends judgments in an attempt to draw the nation back to Himself and also punish the nation's unfaithfulness. Pastor Don shows, with great clarity, that this is exactly what God is now doing with America. The judgments are famine, wild beasts, the sword, and pestilence. This section alone makes *America's Ark* worth reading, as it is sobering to see the hand of God on the nation.

After laying out the condition of America before God, Pastor Don then gives the remedy for living in this hour of American history. The psalmist asks, If the foundations be destroyed, what can the righteous do? (Psalm 11:3)

Pastor Don, in such an enlightening way, answers this question! The answer is Christians are to live with the righteousness of Noah, Daniel, and Job! With great insights, Pastor Don brings fresh revelations to the character of these three great men and how to make them relevant to today. He shows how to make their characteristics your characteristics.

America's Ark is the book for the hour in which we live. It is like a spiritual manual for living and pleasing the Lord for modern American Christians. The book is a must read for the spiritual riches and truths it reveals. It should be taught in Sunday schools across the nation. After reading this book, your walk with the Lord will never be the same.

Great job, Pastor Don.
John P. McTernan, Ph.D

Preface

S ince my years as a child back in the 1960s during the "Jesus Movement"—you may remember "Jesus is far out man"—I have been hearing about Bible prophecy and the return of our Lord Jesus. Having come back to the Lord in 1995, after many wilderness years, I must make a pretty significant claim: "The reality of the things you will find in *America's Ark* will be the only reliable refuge for any human being in America and on the planet in this twenty-first century!" You can quote me on it.

How can one make such a claim? There is a military term used today called "red lines." It means that when these boundaries are crossed, a nation's military goes into action. The God of the Bible has certain clearly marked red lines, and they have been breached for years by America. Now, the true and living God is moving as a Man of War, and there is nothing anyone can do to stop Him!

It is not that God has declared war on America, but that America has declared war on God. The Lord is simply responding to the challenge as, amongst many of His grand attributes, He is a Man of War! One thing is for certain—He is not a mere man that He should lie!

The LORD is a man of war; The LORD is His name. (Exodus 15:3)

His battle plan is precise and has been clearly spelled out through His prophetic word. There are many Bible prophecies that have been taught far and wide, but few so clearly for America as those presented in *America's Ark*. These little-known passages explain the strategies of the Lord Jesus and the way for any who will uncompromisingly follow Him during the troubled days in which we live.

THINK ABOUT THIS:

The Apostle Paul was writing to the church in Ephesus. Through his troubles of mocking, beatings, imprisonment, and more, Paul had something that kept him going which he wanted the church in Ephesus to have as well. He prayed they would receive what made every obstacle and trouble thrown in front of him seem like little nothings:

> . . . that the God of our Lord Jesus Christ, the Father of glory, may give to you the spirit of wisdom and revelation in the knowledge of Him . . . (Ephesians 1:17)

What did Paul have that he desperately wanted for the people of the Lord in his day and ours? He desired them to have wisdom and revelation in the knowledge of our Lord Jesus! Like many down through the centuries I have asked the Lord for such revelation and wisdom and pray it for you in this critical generation, that the things of the Lord from the pages of *America's Ark* would leap into your spirit!

Our only hope now is to know the place of refuge the True and Living God has provided for anyone who seeks cover in today's Ark. When did Noah's family need this floating house of protection? It was during time of catastrophic trouble and uncertainty. This is, and will increasingly become, the most troubled, calamitous, and seemingly uncertain generation in the history of mankind!

In *America's Ark* not only will you find the opportunity to better understand the times in which the Lord has placed you in history—and there are many books that are helping us with that today—but you will also learn the one and only way to the safe haven prepared and prescribed by the Lord Himself through His prophet Ezekiel. There is a passage in Ezekiel's fourteenth chapter nobody is talking about today, and it is increasingly leaping off the pages of the Bible into our everyday lives with each passing moment!

Many news articles will be quoted for the purpose of bringing home the reality of these times. Though they may seem dated by the time you are reading, realize they are just another confirming resource to measure against the scriptures and our times. I am confident the articles that are current while you are reading this book will demonstrate how quickly things are progressing from the time of this writing. The news articles are not the authority to interpret Biblical scripture, but are simply a road marker for the signs of the times.

Chapter 1

Understanding the Times

Of the sons of Issachar who had understanding of the times, to know what Israel ought to do. . . (I Chronicles 12:32)

During the 1990s, I was learning much about Bible prophecy from some of the best teachers on this important subject that is especially critical for our day. It was, and still is, necessary for me to hear, read, and learn about the days in which we live—including world events that culminate with the second coming of our Lord Jesus in the Rapture and His Millennial Reign from Jerusalem. However, I also learned that much of the teaching handed down through the years needed some refining and seemed to lack personal revelation from some teaching the prophetic scenarios. I, too, have certainly been found wanting at times in the personal revelation department, so I am not beating up on anybody.

Here is what I mean: Bible prophecy becomes less mysterious and more clear as it is unfolding. The Lord's Prophet Jeremiah warned Israel they would go into seventy years of captivity in Babylon and then somehow return to Jerusalem. The seventy years those from the Southern Kingdom of Judah would spend in Babylonian and then Persian captivity, along with the completion of the years, became much more clear and understandable to Daniel as they were being completed. The Holy One of Israel revealed what

those seventy years meant to Daniel and his people in the generation of their fulfillment at the end of their captivity:

*"In the first year of his reign I, Daniel, understood by the books
the number of the years specified by the word of the LORD
through Jeremiah the prophet, that He would accomplish seventy years in the desolations of Jerusalem." (Daniel 9:2)*

By way of reminder, according to the prophet's warnings to
Judah for their rebellion and sin, the Babylonians came in, sacked
Jerusalem, and took many captives to Babylon from the Southern
Kingdom of Israel. Then, according to the words given to Daniel
from the Lord, Persia conquered Babylon. Many years earlier, the
Prophet Jeremiah wrote that the Jewish people would return to
Jerusalem from captivity at the end of seventy years, which is
where we picked up in Daniel 9.

Jeremiah's prophecy was not understood as clearly by Daniel
earlier while under Babylonian rule, as it was when the Lord was
bringing it to pass later in Daniel's time under the Persian Empire.
Our Father in Heaven wanted Daniel involved in fasting, praying,
and interceding. He gave the meaning of Jeremiah's prophecy to
Daniel by personal revelation, so he could be an instrument of grace
and mercy during this time of prophetic fulfillment. Dear follower
of Jesus Christ reading this book, that is what our Lord Jesus wants
to do with you and me today in our time of prophetic fulfillment!
Great prophetic events are flying off the pages of the Bible into our
generation, and this is our time to be an instrument of grace and
mercy!

In a similar fashion, Bible prophecy began becoming more clear,
specific, and real to me beginning in the year 2000 and has been
ramping up since. Of course I am not alone as many are hearing
from the Lord Jesus pertaining to these things in this impacting
hour of human history. By our Abba Father's grace, let's not miss
out on our time of fulfillment!

During the summer of 2001 our Lord began waking me up in the
wee hours of the night and morning. There is a Bible passage I had
never considered that tragically became living color that summer by

revelation from the Holy Spirit, and came crashing into our physical world that autumn. Thankfully, in judgment and tragedy, there is grace and mercy. The kindness of God to present a place of refuge is also clearly presented in these verses as the only means of escape for those in our country who will take heed to the word of the Lord. Hence the title is *America's Ark.*

Before giving the entire passage of scripture I will ask a question: Without looking, can you quote anything from Ezekiel 14? I couldn't either until the summer of 2001. But since then I see these verses leaping into everyday life in so many places in our country and the world around us. It is so clear, and I pray you will see them clearly as well.

> *The word of the LORD came again to me, saying: "Son of man, when a land sins against Me by persistent unfaithfulness, I will stretch out My hand against it; I will cut off its supply of bread, send famine on it, and cut off man and beast from it. Even if these three men, Noah, Daniel, and Job, were in it, they would deliver only themselves by their righteousness," says the Lord GOD.*

> *"If I cause wild beasts to pass through the land, and they empty it, and make it so desolate that no man may pass through because of the beasts, even though these three men were in it, as I live," says the Lord GOD, "they would deliver neither sons nor daughters; only they would be delivered, and the land would be desolate.*

> *"Or if I bring a sword on that land, and say, 'Sword, go through the land,' and I cut off man and beast from it, even though these three men were in it, as I live," says the Lord GOD, "they would deliver neither sons nor daughters, but only they themselves would be delivered.*

> *"Or if I send a pestilence into that land and pour out My fury on it in blood, and cut off from it man and beast, even though Noah, Daniel, and Job were in it, as I live," says the Lord GOD, "they*

would deliver neither son nor daughter; they would deliver only themselves by their righteousness." (Ezekiel 14:12–20)

The tears dropped on the pages containing these words in the early morning hours, and I knew the Holy Spirit was warning me that this scenario was for America. Of course, it was initially a warning for Israel and other nations later through the centuries, but I knew that America was in the bull's-eye of this passage. The strong and overwhelming emotions emanating from these passages and what the Lord was about to do were consuming my thoughts. I knew with everything in me, a strong judgment was coming to America. The problem was, as I would tell people who should want to know, they simply did not want to hear it. Things haven't changed much from Isaiah's day:

"Who say to the seers, 'Do not see,' And to the prophets, 'Do not prophesy to us right things; Speak to us smooth things, prophesy deceits.'" (Isaiah 30:10)

Now, I am not calling myself a prophet or the son of a prophet, but I knew from the Lord Jesus that a strong judgment was coming and like those in Isaiah's day, the people did not want to hear of judgment in 2001 in America—only smooth sayings would do for the people of God with whom I would speak—including some pastors!

And my testimony of those in the Lord who knew something tragic was around the corner was not isolated. Many were preparing, though they were not sure exactly what was coming. I remember David Wilkerson's ministry was mobilizing people for prayer and other preparations at Times Square Church in New York City to be ready for something big in their own back yard.

For an example of people who did not want to listen, I will share a testimony of a scenario that took place in August 2001. I was asked to speak at a large Bible Study at a large church in a large city—Houston, Texas. I taught on some of these things and said: "The Lord is about to take us to the woodshed, and I don't want to go there!" The response was quite disappointing and scaled from disinterest to tangible anger. Few, if any, got it and frankly, it was sad to watch.

So, finally the day came, September 11, 2001. My wife and I were having a lively discussion regarding Israel and America. I was telling her that before long it would be safer for us in Israel than America. As a Jewish believer in Jesus with many believing friends in Israel, we talk about the Promised Land in my house quite frequently. My wife couldn't understand how I could say something so foolish while buses were blowing up all over Jerusalem during the Arab uprising or "intifada." My mother was almost killed one day, but did not get on the bus that blew up thirty meters away as it pulled off from where she stood. So, I showed my wife these verses and closed my Bible when the phone rang.

A dear family friend and lover of Israel, was calling and urgently told me to turn on the television— "We have been hit by a terrorist attack in New York City!" I turned on the TV and saw the smoldering building from the first plane, and I began walking up and down the hallway of our home saying: "There is more, it is not over!" And then the next plane, and I continued pacing saying "There is still more, it is still not over!" And of course there was more. Dear Americans, and all others who will listen, "There is more, it is STILL NOT OVER!" We need to get in *America's Ark*!

Chapter 2

But They Are Not

If My people who are called by My name will humble them-
selves, and pray and seek My face . . . (2 Chronicles 7:14)

The event called 9/11 was unlike anything that has ever taken place in modern America or the world, for that matter. The scenario is etched into people's minds across the country and around the globe. Not only were Americans shocked, fear and borderline widespread panic understandably gripped society. I remember apprehensively seeing planes overhead that had just been released to carry passengers after the flight suspension enacted due to concern the once friendly skies were still facilitating civilian manned missiles with wings.

Another important observation, especially from the perspective of a born-again follower of Jesus Christ, is that the long-awaited American revival so desperately hoped for by some pastors and faithful believers appeared to have begun. The anticipation of some was that after so many years of sitting back and watching our country spiral downwards with little concern, and such lukewarmness among professing followers of our Lord Jesus, certainly this would shake us out of our hammocks!

So many indicators seemed to point the direction of potential revival. Churches were filled, people were praying intensely, those who had not been in church were returning. And here is the verse that was heard in churches, television and radio programs, and street corners:

"When I shut up heaven and there is no rain, or command the locusts to devour the land, or send pestilence among My people, if My people who are called by My name will humble themselves, and pray and seek My face, and turn from their wicked ways, then I will hear from heaven, and will forgive their sin and heal their land." (2 Chronicles 7:13–14)

This is a passage of scripture given to Israel that would bring the mercy of the Lord during time of His great judgment on His disobedient people. In these verses we see that the Creator uses His creation to get their attention and punish disobedience as they have offended the Lord by their dark ways. In this case He sent drought and locusts to bring thirst and hunger for a people who had forgotten to hunger and thirst for righteousness. He also brought pestilence, which is disease that will be explained more clearly later in this book. They had forgotten their Sustainer and Healer, and these things were important reminders.

Graciously and mercifully, though they had greatly offended their loving Creator the Holy One of Israel, He prescribed the cure for His people's problems in that they must: humble themselves, pray, seek His face, turn from their wicked ways, and then He would hear from heaven, forgive their sin, and heal their land. This verse was offered to Americans from shore to shore—boundary to boundary.

Sadly, after about three to six weeks with no more tragedy from the terrorists, the truth about this superficial revival became all too clear. The churches emptied out, mostly back to the attendance of their pre-9/11 congregants, as most of the short lived increase evaporated and business as usual overcame the professing, yet not behaving Christ-like, Christians in America. It was a very sad thing to watch, and it still is.

You see, when revival breaks out, believers in Jesus Christ become very sensitive about their own sin, and the Lord Jesus grants them great repentance. There is an overwhelming and powerful sense of His presence that bursts out past the walls of the church building into the lives of sinners in the community! The lost get saved, and the community is impacted in that they too have a sense of sin and a great desire for righteousness.

Historically during times of revival, bar owners have shut down their dark establishments and gotten saved by Jesus, prostitutes repented and became women of God, lazy selfish church members, concerned for the souls of men, began to preach the gospel! Churches filled up because the Holy Spirit of the living God was there in clear and tangible ways! Is that what you see today in churches and the surrounding communities?

The problem is that this verse is still spoken today as if the professing believers in Messiah Jesus who would not repent with the nation shaking and trembling under the weight of 9/11 would somehow do so when everything seems fine. The reality is most are not going to read or hear this verse and take a 180-degree turn away from habitual unrighteousness. Tragically, we have gone too far up the road past 2 Chronicles 7:14—it is not going to happen without further judgment.

"With my soul have I desired thee in the night; yea, with my spirit within me will I seek thee early: for when thy judgments are in the earth, the inhabitants of the world will learn righteousness." (Isaiah 26:9)

That is not to say that individuals, individual churches, and even cities or regions cannot catch fire for the gospel at any moment. Yet, though there be pockets of revival this is the time of the great apostasy, or falling away from the truth of the gospel, spoken of in 2 Thessalonians chapter 2 in the New Testament. Rejection of the truth of the Lord is apostasy and is sweeping across churches in America and the world, as it is a "sign of the times" that points to the return of our Lord Jesus Christ.

Chapter 3

The Lord's Founding
and Establishing of America

Blessed is the nation whose God is the LORD, The people He has chosen as His own inheritance. (Psalm 33:12)

*T*here is so much historical and contemporary literature proving and explaining the Biblical nature of America's founding, which is sadly and conveniently ignored, that I will not be exhaustive in exploring the subject. But let's take a brief walk through history to remind us of our heavenly heritage. Of course, there have been many historical sins that have plagued this land and even caused a horrific Civil War. However, America has been founded on Biblical Old and New Testament principles, and the lives of many impacted by this foundation have made America faithful in its founding and much of its history like none other.

The purpose of this and the next chapter is to give us a comparison of a land that was, to a much greater degree than it is today, faithful to the Lord.

1600s—Puritans

The Puritans who originally came to America did so to escape the religious tyranny of the Church of England. They wanted to have the freedom to interpret the Bible with autonomy and live out its pages in pursuit of advancing the Kingdom of God. Later in sects of the Puritan movement, and for us historically, we see the good, bad, and the ugly. However, there is no doubt their original charter was to come to this land to be good citizens, first of the Kingdom of God, and then to establish a land that was faithful to its Creator. And to a great degree that is what they accomplished.

> *On this day in 1630, the last well-wishers stepped off the ship Arabella and returned to shore. More than a week after the vessel first set out, the winds were finally favorable. The ship weighed anchor and sailed for New England. Governor John Winthrop and approximately 300 English Puritans were on board. They were leaving their homes in England to settle in a fledgling colony—Massachusetts Bay—on the other side of the Atlantic. There they would work "to do more service to the Lord." Governor Winthrop shepherded the Puritans through 12 years of enormous hardship. Under his leadership, Massachusetts Bay became the most populous English colony and Boston the largest city in North America.*[1]

1700s

The Colonies:

The Colonies that laid the foundation for this land were also founded with the Kingdom of the God of the Bible in the forefront. Due to the brevity of this perusal through the generations I will list only part of one colonial charter and another's constitution.

Delaware Charter 1701

BECAUSE no People can be truly happy, though under the greatest Enjoyment of Civil Liberties, if abridged of the Freedom of their Consciences, as to their Religious Profession and Worship: And Almighty God being the only Lord of Conscience, Father of Lights and Spirits; and the Author as well as Object of all divine Knowledge, Faith and Worship, who only doth enlighten the Minds, and persuade and convince the Understandings of People, I do hereby grant and declare, That no Person or Persons, inhabiting In this Province or Territories, who shall confess and acknowledge One almighty God, the Creator, Upholder and Ruler of the World; and professes him or themselves obliged to live quietly under the Civil Government, shall be in any Case molested or prejudiced, in his or their Person or Estate, because of his or their conscientious Persuasion or Practice, nor be compelled to frequent or maintain any religious Worship, Place or Ministry, contrary to his or their Mind, or to do or suffer any other Act or Thing, contrary to their religious Persuasion.

AND that all Persons who also profess to believe in Jesus Christ, the Saviour of the World, shall be capable (notwithstanding their other Persuasions and Practices in Point of Conscience and Religion) to serve this Government in any Capacity, both legislatively and executively, he or they solemnly promising, when lawfully required, Allegiance to the King as Sovereign, and Fidelity to the Proprietary and Governor, and taking the Attests as now established by the Law made at Newcastle, in the Year One Thousand and Seven Hundred, entitled, An Act directing the Attests of several Officers and Ministers, as now amended and confirmed this present Assembly.[2]

Constitution of Maryland—November 11, 1776

XXXIII. That, as it is the duty of every man to worship God in such manner as he thinks most acceptable to him; all persons, professing the Christian religion, are equally entitled to protection in their religious liberty; wherefore no person ought by any law to be molested in his person or estate on account of his religious persuasion or profession, or for his religious practice; unless, under colour of religion, any man shall disturb the good order, peace or safety of the State, or shall infringe the laws of morality, or injure others, in their natural, civil, or religious rights; nor ought any person to be compelled to frequent or maintain, or contribute, unless on contract, to maintain any particular place of worship, or any particular ministry; yet the Legislature may, in their discretion, lay a general and equal tax for the support of the Christian religion; leaving to each individual the power of appointing the payment over of the money, collected from him, to the support of any particular place of worship or minister, or for the benefit of the poor of his own denomination, or the poor in general of any particular county: but the churches, chapels, globes, and all other property now belonging to the church of England, ought to remain to the church of England forever.[3]

U.S. Constitution

Contrary to the absurd assertions of the revisionists of our generation, the U.S. Constitution, along with other founding documents, were greatly influenced by faithful men whose aspirations were to live in a land that was faithful to the Lord Jesus Christ. Many of the Constitutional signers were fervent born-again Christians. There were also those who did not profess born-again faith, but the Bible was a significant part of their lives and influenced their governing philosophies.

This List of signers certainly is an undeniable witness (those highlighted were of special interest to me personally):

- Baldwin, Abraham—Chaplain in the American Revolution (Delegate to Constitutional Convention, Signer of Constitution)
- **Bassett, Richard**—Participated in writing the Constitution of Delaware, which states: "Every person who shall be chosen a member of either house, or appointed to any office or place of trust . . . shall . . . make and subscribe the following declaration, to wit: 'I, ____, do profess faith in God the Father, and in Jesus Christ His only Son, and in the Holy Ghost, one God, blessed for evermore; and I do acknowledge the holy scriptures of the Old and New Testament to be given by divine inspiration.'" (Delegate to Constitutional Convention, Signer of Constitution)

- **Bedford, Gunning**—Funeral oration on the death of Washington: "Now to the triune God, The Father, the Son, and the Holy Ghost, be ascribed all honor and dominion, forevermore." (Delegate to Constitutional Convention, Signer of Constitution)
- Blair, John—Member of the Episcopal Church (Delegate to Constitutional Convention, Signer of Constitution)
- **Blount, William**—Member of the Presbyterian Church. Helped draft the Tennessee Constitution, which said, "No person who denies the being of God, or a future state of rewards and punishments, shall hold any office in the civil department of this State." (Delegate to Constitutional Convention, Signer of Constitution)
- Brearly, David—A warden of St. Michael's Church, a compiler of the Protestant Episcopal Prayer Book, and a delegate to the Episcopal General Convention in 1786 (Delegate to Constitutional Convention, Signer of Constitution)
- **Broom, Jacob**—Writing to his son: "Don't forget to be a Christian. I have said much to you on this head and I hope an indelible impression is made." (Delegate to Constitutional Convention, Signer of Constitution)
- Butler, Pierce—Member of the Episcopal Church (Delegate to Constitutional Convention, Signer of Constitution)
- Carroll, Daniel—A Catholic who studied under the Jesuits at the College of St. Omer in Flanders (one of two Roman Catholics to sign the Constitution) (Delegate to Constitutional Convention, Signer of Constitution)
- Clymer, George—Was both a Quaker and an Episcopalian (Signer of Declaration of Independence, Delegate to Constitutional Convention, Signer of Constitution)
- Dayton, Jonathan—Member of the Episcopal Church (Delegate to Constitutional Convention, Signer of Constitution)
- **Dickinson, John**—From his will: "To my Creator I resign myself, humbly confiding in His goodness and in His mercy through Jesus Christ for the events of eternity." (Delegate to Constitutional Convention, Signer of Constitution)

- Few, William—Few was a devout Methodist and was known to donate generously to philanthropic causes. (Delegate to Constitutional Convention, Signer of Constitution)
- Fitzsimons, Thomas—Member of the Roman Catholic Church (Delegate to Constitutional Convention, Signer of Constitution)
- **Franklin, Benjamin**—Considered much more a Deist than a Christian. He was nonetheless a follower of the Bible, and said: "I have lived, sir, a long time, and the longer I live, the more convincing proofs I see of this truth—God Governs in the Affairs of Men, And if a Sparrow cannot fall to the ground without His notice, Is it possible that an empire can rise without His aid? . . . Except the Lord build the house, They labor in vain who build it." (Delegate to Constitutional Convention, Signer of Constitution)
- Gilman, Nicholas—Gilman was a Congregationalist. (Delegate to Constitutional Convention, Signer of Constitution)
- Gorham, Nathaniel—A Congregationalist who helped write the Massachusetts's Constitution, which required this in the oath for office: " . . . I believe the Christian religion, and have a firm persuasion of its truth." (Delegate to Constitutional Convention, Signer of Constitution)
- **Hamilton, Alexander**—Proposed formation of the Christian Constitutional Society to spread Christian government around the world. After the Constitutional Convention of 1787, he stated: "For my own part, I sincerely esteem it a system which without the finger of God, never could have been suggested and agreed upon by such a diversity of interests."—from Diffine, D.P., *One Nation Under God—How Close a Separation?* (Delegate to Constitutional Convention, Signer of Constitution)
- Ingersoll, Jared—Member of the Presbyterian Church (Delegate to Constitutional Convention, Signer of Constitution)
- **Johnson, William Samuel**—Speaking as president of Columbia University to the first graduating class after the Revolutionary War: "Remember, too, that you are the redeemed of the Lord, that you are bought with a price, even the inestimable price

of the precious blood of the Son of God." (Delegate to Constitutional Convention, Signer of Constitution)

- **King, Rufus**—Selected as manager of the American Bible Society. In a speech made before the Senate at the time Missouri was petitioning for statehood, he said: "I hold that all laws or compacts imposing any such condition [as involuntary servitude] upon any human being are absolutely void because contrary to the law of nature, which is the law of God." (Delegate to Constitutional Convention, Signer of Constitution)

- **Langdon, John**—Vice president of the American Bible Society (Delegate to Constitutional Convention, Signer of Constitution)

- Livingston, William—Said, "I believe the Scriptures of the Old and New Testaments, without any foreign comments or human explanations . . . I believe that he who feareth God and worketh righteousness will be accepted of Him . . ." (Delegate to Constitutional Convention, Signer of Constitution)

- **Madison, James**—Member of the Episcopal Church. He said, "The belief in a God, all powerful, wise, and good, [is] essential to the moral order of the world, and to the happiness of man." (Signer of Declaration of Independence, Delegate to Constitutional Convention, Signer of Constitution)

- **McHenry, James**—President of the first Bible Society in Baltimore. In soliciting funds for distribution of Bibles, he wrote: ". . . Consider also, the rich do not possess aught more precious than their Bible, and that the poor cannot be presented by the rich with anything of greater value." (Delegate to Constitutional Convention, Signer of Constitution)

- Mifflin, Thomas—Known as both a Quaker and a Lutheran (Delegate to Constitutional Convention, Signer of Constitution)

- Morris, Governor—"The most important of all lessons [from the Scriptures] is the denunciation of ruin to every State that rejects the precepts of religion." (Delegate to Constitutional Convention, Signer of Constitution)

- Morris, Robert—Member of the Episcopal Church (Signer of Declaration of Independence, Delegate to Constitutional Convention, Signer of Constitution)
- Paterson, William—Supreme Court Justice and a signer of the Constitution, declared that "Religion and morality . . . [are] necessary to good government, good order, and good laws"; (Delegate to Constitutional Convention, Signer of Constitution)
- **Pinckney, Charles Cotesworth**—President of the Charleston Bible Society; vice president of the American Bible Society (Delegate to Constitutional Convention, Signer of Constitution)
- Read, George—Read was an Episcopalian. (Signer of Declaration of Independence, Signer of Constitution)
- Rutledge, John—Member of the Episcopal Church (Delegate to Constitutional Convention, Signer of Constitution)
- **Sherman, Roger**—(Signer of all four of our founding documents). When asked by his church, White Haven Congregational, to help revise the wording of their creed: "I believe that there is one only living and true God, existing in three persons, the Father, the Son, and the Holy Ghost, the same in substance, equal in power and glory. That the Scriptures of the old and new testaments are a revelation from God and a complete rule to direct us how we may glorify and enjoy Him." (Delegate to Constitutional Convention, Signer of Constitution)
- Spaight, Richard Dobbs—Member of the Episcopal Church (Delegate to Constitutional Convention, Signer of Constitution)
- **Washington, George**—Member of the Episcopal Church. In his prayer at Valley Forge he said, "Almighty and eternal Lord God, the great Creator of heaven and earth, and the God and Father of our Lord Jesus Christ; look down from heaven in pity and compassion upon me Thy servant, who humbly prorate myself before Thee." (Delegate to Constitutional Convention, Signer of Constitution)
- **Wilson, James**—Wilson was an Episcopalian and a Presbyterian. Supreme Court Justice. He declared that "Human law

must rest its authority ultimately upon the authority of that law which is Divine . . . Far from being rivals or enemies, religion and law are twin sisters, friends, and mutual assistants." (Delegate to Constitutional Convention, Signer of Constitution)

- **Witherspoon, John**—Witherspoon was a Presbyterian. He said, "Shun, as a contagious pestilence, . . . those especially whom you perceive to be infected with the principles of infidelity or [who are] enemies to the power of religion." (Signer of Declaration of Independence, Signer of Constitution)[4]

Declaration of Independence

Regarding the signers of the Declaration of Independence, the same holds true in terms of their Biblical faith and morality that characterized their lives. So, to briefly make the point here is a well-known quote that established this land we call America:

"We hold these truths to be self-evident, that all men are created equal, that they are endowed by their Creator with certain unalienable Rights, that among these are Life, Liberty and the pursuit of Happiness."[5]

The Founders of this Constitutional Republic knew that our Creator Jesus Christ gave Americans rights from which no man could alienate us as this land was founded upon His word and ways. There has never been, since Israel, a land that could embrace such principles, as they were not founded on God's word—nothing in the world like America!

President George Washington

In response to Indians in Delaware requesting educational opportunities for their children, listen to George Washington: *"You do well to wish to learn our arts and our ways of life **and above all, the religion of Jesus Christ**. These will make you a greater and hap-*

pier people than you are. Congress will do everything they can to assist you in this wise intention."[6]

According to George Washington, what students would learn in American schools "above all" was "the religion of Jesus Christ."

Thomas Jefferson was America's second Vice President and third President. James Madison was our nation's fourth President. Once again hear the words of yesterday's American statesmen and be reminded of leaders who were more faithful to principles of life and freedom.

Thomas Jefferson wrote: *"God who gave us life gave us liberty. And can the liberties of a nation be thought secure when we have removed their only firm basis, a conviction in the minds of the people that these liberties are a gift from God? That they are not to be violated but with His wrath? **Indeed I tremble for my country when I reflect that God is just, and that His justice cannot sleep forever."*[7]

> *"We've staked our future on our ability to follow the Ten Commandments with all of our heart."—James Madison, 1778, to the General Assembly of the State of Virginia.*[8]

America's First Supreme Court Chief Justice John Jay

> *"Providence has given to our people the choice of their rulers, and it is the duty, as well as the privilege and interest of our Christian nation to select and prefer Christians for their rulers."*[9]

National Monuments

Our National Monuments proclaim upon whose shoulders this land stands and whose favor we so desperately need:

> *Judges and legislators who exhibit confusion about the constitutionality of acknowledgments of God in (and on) public buildings should get out of their stuffy chambers and go visit some of our national treasures. Just one day spent traversing the Mall in Washington, D.C., would expose them to an undeniable fact*

of American history: Biblical and religious quotations, including the Ten Commandments, adorn nearly every significant building and monument in our nation's capital, inscribed and enshrined there as the natural public conversation of America's leaders in every generation. Indeed, the role of faith, family and freedom in American history is inscribed on monuments across the length and breadth of Washington, D.C. For instance, the words of Lincoln's Second Inaugural Address, carved in granite, thunder from inside the Memorial that bears his name, praying that the "mighty scourge of war may speedily pass away" but recalling that "the judgments of the Lord are true and righteous altogether." From the Lincoln Memorial, a perfect line of sight connects you with the magnificent obelisk of the Washington Monument. The form of the Monument recalls ancient Rome and Greece, but at its topmost point, inscribed on the aluminum tip of the capstone, is the Latin phrase Laus Deo—"Praise be to God." Along the stairway to that height are 190 carved tributes donated by states, cities, individuals, associations, and foreign governments. The blocks resound with quotations from Scripture—"Holiness to the Lord" (Exodus 28), "Search the Scriptures" (John 5:39), "The memory of the just is blessed" (Proverbs 10:7)—and such invocations as, "May Heaven to this Union continue its Benefice. [10]

Along with the writings, monuments, and lives that expressed Biblical faith that founded America, we see how a nation founded upon the God of the Bible was led to turn and ask for mercy from the One who gives grace and mercy in time of crisis:

1800s—A Portion of President Abraham Lincoln's National Day of Prayer Proclamation:

President Abraham Lincoln's Proclamation: A Day of National Humiliation, Fasting, and Prayer in the United States of America on April 30, 1863

WHEREAS, the senate of the United States, devoutly recognizing the Supreme Authority and Just Government of Almighty God, in all the affairs of men and of nations, has by a resolution, required the President to designate and set apart a day for National prayer and humiliation:

And whereas, it is the duty of nations as well as of men, to owe their dependence upon the overruling power of God, to con-

fess their sins and transgressions, in humble sorrow, yet with assured hope that genuine repentance will lead to mercy and pardon; and to recognize the sublime truth, announced in the Holy Scriptures and proven by all history, that those nations only are blessed whose God is the Lord:

And, in so much as we know that, by His divine law, nations, like individuals, are subjected to punishments and chastisements in this world, may we not justly fear that the awful calamity of civil war, which now desolates the land, may be but a punishment inflicted upon us for our presumptuous sins, to the needful end of our national reformation as a whole People? We have been the recipients of the choicest bounties of Heaven. We have been preserved, these many years, in peace and prosperity. We have grown in numbers, wealth, and power as no other nation has ever grown. But we have forgotten God. We have forgotten the gracious hand which preserved us in peace, and multiplied and enriched and strengthened us; and we have vainly imagined, in the deceitfulness of our hearts, that all these blessings were produced by some superior wisdom and virtue of our own. Intoxicated with unbroken success, we have become too self-sufficient to feel the necessity of redeeming and preserving grace, too proud to pray to the God that made us! It behooves us, then to humble ourselves before the offended Power, to confess our national sins, and to pray for clemency and forgiveness.[11]

These evidences only scratch the surface of all the readily available information shouting out that a land called America was founded and established on and by the Judeo-Christian faith in our Lord Jesus Christ!

Please continue with me on this brief, yet refreshing walk through our nations' more faithful days.

Chapter 4

Education, the Family, and the Evangelical Christian Religion in Early America

You shall teach them [Biblical Principles]
diligently to your children . . . (Deuteronomy 6:7)

*T*he way a society is shaped and established rests upon the foundation of how it educates those who will shape and establish the culture of the future. These young minds and lives are intentionally taught principles based on philosophies either of the Lord Jesus Christ or those of man. These children then grow into society's positions intentionally prepared to define culture and actually become the promoters of those philosophies and principles locally, regionally, nationally, and beyond.

What were the first principles taught to American children? What was the curriculum that expressed the philosophies and principles that were intentionally given to children in America to shape its society? And remember, these ideas affect everything in the culture: family, education, government, legal system, military, media, entertainment, EVERYTHING!

The Bible was often taught at home, church, and in schools in early America. The family is where the children were first educated and then school. The family was traditionally a cohesive unit of love, care, diligent work, and upbringing.

What was the first book taught in schools in America?

"As part of the daily curriculum, students were taught to pray and read using the Bible. Later in 1690 the New England Primer was introduced which taught spelling, reading and the Alphabet using Bible verses, thus teaching both reading and Bible morals at the same time."[1]

William Holmes McGuffey was a Professor of Languages at Miami University in Oxford Ohio during the 1800s. His McGuffey Readers provided all the most important academic subjects along with Biblical doctrines and principles. The children educated by these important American educational tools not only received important academic knowledge and skills—they additionally learned to honor God, tell the truth, the ills of stealing, lying, cheating, gluttony, foul language, and so on.

Two of the best-known school books in the history of American education were the 18th century New England Primer and the 19th century McGuffey Readers. Of the two, McGuffey's was the most popular and widely used. It is estimated that at least 120 million copies of McGuffey's Readers were sold between 1836 and 1960, placing its sales in a category with the Bible and Webster's Dictionary. Since 1961 they have continued to sell at a rate of some 30,000 copies a year. No other textbook bearing a single person's name has come close to that mark. McGuffey's Readers are still in use today in some school systems, and by parents for home schooling purposes. [2]

Rev. William Holmes McGuffey had already planned a series of readers and had published his first reader. This first reader of 1841 introduces children to McGuffey's ethical code. The child modeled in this book is prompt, good, kind, honest and truthful. This first book contained fifty-five lessons.

The second reader appeared simultaneously with the first and followed the same pattern. It contained reading and spelling with eighty-five lessons, sixteen pictures and one-hundred sixty-six pages. It outlined history, biology, astronomy, zoology, botany; table manners, behavior towards family, attitudes toward God and teachers, the poor; the great and the good. The duties of youth are stressed. Millions of pioneer men and women were alumni of this second reader college, they were able to read and write English. The third reader was much more formal. It contained rules for oral reading of its fifty-seven lessons. This book contained only three pictures and was designed for a more mature mind, of junior high standing today. The fourth reader was an introduction to good literature. It contained British poetry and used the Bible among its selections. This text was addressed to the highest grade in schools, its difficulty compared to that of American secondary schools. It discussed Napoleon Bonaparte, Puritan fathers, women, God, education, religion and philosophy. [3]

Think about this incredible article as you listen to the quotes from Noah Webster:

Noah Webster, the Father of American Education, was a revolutionary soldier, judge, legislator, American Founder, and the creator of Webster's Dictionary. He served nine terms in the Connecticut General Assembly, three terms in the Massachusetts Legislature, and four years as a judge. One of the first Founding Fathers to call for a Constitutional Convention, he was also one of the most active in the ratification of the Constitution.

As evidenced in his textbook, History of the United States, *published in 1832, he believed that Christianity and government could not and should not be separated:*

The religion which has introduced civil liberty is the religion of Christ and His apostles, which enjoins humility, piety, and benevolence; which acknowledges in every person, a brother or a sister, and a citizen with equal rights. This is genuine Christianity, and to this we owe our free constitutions of government.

He is also quoted as saying:

Every civil government is based upon some religion or philosophy of life. Education in a nation will propagate the religion of that nation. In America, the foundational religion was Christianity. And it was sown in the hearts of Americans through the home and private and public schools for centuries. Our liberty, growth, and prosperity were the result of a Biblical philosophy of life. Our continued freedom and success is dependent on our educating the youth of America in the principles of Christianity.[4]

Think of it: even the children who did not grow up as dedicated Bible readers and followers were affected by the Bible and its principles in a way that preserved society from the natural sinful inclinations that have destroyed societies through the centuries! There was an ethic that permeated all the major elements of society I mentioned above—family, government, legal system, and so on. That being the case, there was an order in society and also a stigma attached with corruption. I am not naïve or foolish enough to think corruption did not exist; I am saying there was a stigma attached to it. There was a society-wide general acceptance of right and wrong according to the philosophies and principles that come from the God of the Bible, Jesus Christ!

Higher Learning

Think of this: some of the oldest colleges founded in America were established upon the Bible and promoted the things of God. Again, hear the history ring true that this land was once faithful:

Most of the colleges in the United States that started over 300 years ago were Bible-proclaiming schools originally. Harvard and Yale (originally Puritan) and Princeton (originally Presbyterian) once had rich Christian histories. Harvard was named after a Christian minister. Yale was started by clergymen, and Princeton's first year of class was taught by Reverend Jonathan Dickinson. Princeton's crest still says "Dei sub numine viget," which is Latin for "Under God she flourishes. [5]

Can you imagine a society in which, from the beginning, children learned the Bible and the ways of Jesus Christ all through college? What special churches and a special society that environment created. The people would come together on Sunday mornings and then the rest of the week would be in a much more conducive atmosphere to live out what they had professed together in their churches.

There was a Frenchman whose well-known quotes say it nicely. Alexis de Tocqueville was a French political thinker and historian who wrote *Democracy in America* in 1835, which was based on observations during his extensive travels in the United States. Though you may have heard some of these oft-quoted sayings from his writings, it certainly is appropriate for the context of this chapter. Speaking of Evangelical Churches and the way their Biblical faith was at the heart of America's success, he said,

> *I sought for the greatness and genius of America in her commodious harbors and her ample rivers—and it was not there . . . in her fertile fields and boundless forests and it was not there . . . in her rich mines and her vast world commerce—and it was not there . . . in her democratic Congress and her matchless Constitution—and it was not there. Not until I went into the churches of America and heard her pulpits flame with righteousness did I understand the secret of her genius and power. America is great because she is good, and if America ever ceases to be good, she will cease to be great.* [6]*

> *Upon my arrival in the United States the religious aspect of the country was the first thing that struck my attention; and the longer I stayed there, the more I perceived the great political consequences resulting from this new state of things. In France I had almost always seen the spirit of religion and the spirit of*

freedom marching in opposite directions. But in America I found they were intimately united and that they reigned in common over the same country.. [7]

There is no doubt about it; America has historically been blessed. It has even risen to the heights of world power status because of the Biblical foundations on which it was placed by the true and living Creator who raises up empires and brings them crashing down!

Chapter 5

The Big Three

. . . According to the abominations of the nations whom the LORD had cast out before the children of Israel. (2 Kings 21:2)

Before looking at contemporary America in comparison to that of days gone by, it may be helpful to step back and seek some understanding about a few things. In the Bible we can see clear patterns in terms of what really upsets the true and living Creator of the Universe—God The Father, God The Son, and God The Holy Spirit. I call a few of the most egregious offenses "The Big Three." For any one of these the LORD would judge nations and bring great destruction upon their land.

1) Shedding Innocent Blood

In God's word, the Bible, we find that the LORD is for the weak. That is where we get the philosophy in this constitutional republic that the rights of the one are as important as the rights of the majority. The USA is a constitutional republic, not solely a democracy. So, the rights of the weak such as fatherless children, widows, the poor, and ethnic minorities, are clearly to be protected from the view of the true and living God. The LORD hates the spilling of innocent blood, which pollutes a land that tolerates it.

Cain and Abel

Then the LORD said to Cain, "Where is Abel your brother?" He said, "I do not know. Am I my brother's keeper?" And He said, "What have you done? The voice of your brother's blood cries out to Me from the ground. So now you are cursed from the earth, which has opened its mouth to receive your brother's blood from your hand. (Genesis 4:9–11)

Babies

*T*hey served their idols, Which became a snare to them. They even sacrificed their sons And their daughters to demons, And shed innocent blood, The blood of their sons and daughters, Whom they sacrificed to the idols of Canaan; And the land was polluted with blood. (Psalm 106:36)

We see from the Bible a great curse is upon a land that sheds innocent blood, and that we are to be very careful with the weakest amongst us. The great thing about it from the perspective of the weak is that ultimately there is no lasting success for the oppressors or endless withholding of justice for the weak. And those made righteous in Messiah Jesus will dwell with Him forever!

I know that the LORD will maintain The cause of the afflicted, And justice for the poor. Surely the righteous shall give thanks to Your name; The upright shall dwell in Your presence. (Psalm 140:12–13)

2) Homosexuality

Before treading into the truth about this issue I must say that there are people who really believe they are standing for justice and good old American values when they take a stand for this hotly contested lifestyle. There are well-meaning individuals, for whom the Merciful Messiah came to save, that stand on the side of legitimizing same sex relationships and even marriage.

I used to strongly believe in many causes that were in direct opposition to my Creator and Lord Messiah Jesus until He saved me and then gave me His world view. I pray for amazing grace to bring understanding and a fear of the Lord to these precious souls. Sadly, the *Homosexual Movement* has become a large and sweeping trend that has duped many. I pray many "come out" from it when they see the truth.

Contrary to what many assert—the clear warning from the God of the Bible, not only in the Old but also in the New Testament, is to have nothing to do with this sin. In the New Testament, we see same-sex relations as an expression of God's wrath in that He turns people over to their own unrestrained dark inclinations. Homosexuality is in a list of sins that demonstrates the godlessness of a society. The Lord Jesus removes His life saving light and darkness quickly is vacuumed in to replace it. For this reason, even many of those who do not personally participate in this sin are involved in the sin of supporting it.

> *"For the wrath of God is revealed from heaven against all ungodliness and unrighteousness of men, who suppress the truth in unrighteousness, because what may be known of God is manifest in them, for God has shown it to them." (Romans 1:18–19)*

> *"Therefore God also gave them up to uncleanness, in the lusts of their hearts, to dishonor their bodies among themselves, who exchanged the truth of God for the lie, and worshiped and served the creature rather than the Creator, who is blessed forever. Amen." (Romans 1:24–25)*

> *"For this reason God gave them up to vile passions. For even their women exchanged the natural use for what is against nature. Likewise also the men, leaving the natural use of the woman, burned in their lust for one another, men with men committing what is shameful, and receiving in themselves the penalty of their error which was due." (Romans 1:26–27)*

And even as they did not like to retain God in their knowledge, God gave them over to a debased mind, to do those things which are not fitting; being filled with all unrighteousness, sexual immorality, wickedness, covetousness, maliciousness; full of envy, murder, strife, deceit, evil-mindedness; they are whisperers, backbiters, haters of God, violent, proud, boasters, inventors of evil things, disobedient to parents, undiscerning, untrustworthy, unloving, unforgiving, unmerciful; who, knowing the righteous judgment of God, that those who practice such things are deserving of death, not only do the same but also approve of those who practice them. (Romans 1:28–32)

It is important to remind professing Jesus followers that the judgment is from God not people who follow our Lord, meaning we are to tell and warn with the truth in love. We who have been saved by the grace of God the Father should feel great sorrow over others who are perishing—even warning them at the risk of being hated and called names.

In another place in the New Testament there is a warning that is unimaginably becoming more timely and necessary for us to hear and know. You cannot be a homosexual and a born-again Christian. You can be a former homosexual and a born-again Christian, but not a practicing one who believes that it is not sin and is even approved of by the Lord. In this dark hour it is becoming more common to hear of practicing homosexuals asserting their "faith" in Jesus Christ. If I have to choose between believing them or the Bible, and we do, my decision is obvious:

"Do you not know that the unrighteous will not inherit the kingdom of God? Do not be deceived. Neither fornicators, nor idolaters, nor adulterers, nor homosexuals, nor sodomites, nor thieves, nor covetous, nor drunkards, nor revilers, nor extortioners will inherit the kingdom of God. And such were some of you. But you were washed, but you were sanctified, but you were justified in the name of the Lord Jesus and by the Spirit of our God." (1 Corinthians 6:9–11)

3) Cursing Israel (The BIGGEST of the Big Three!)

The true and living God also calls Himself the Holy One of Israel. He does so because the covenant He made with Abraham was passed to Isaac, and then Jacob (Genesis 17:19, 28:13–15). The God of Jacob then changed Jacob's name to Israel (Genesis 32:28), which means Prince of God. We see the terms of the covenant in the seven promises the LORD made with Abram— later Abraham.

Now the LORD had said to Abram: "Get out of your country, From your family And from your father's house, To a land that I will show you. I will make you a great nation; I will bless you And make your name great; And you shall be a blessing. I will bless those who bless you, And I will curse him who curses you; And in you all the families of the earth shall be blessed." (Genesis 12:1–3)

There is great blessing and cursing associated with the treatment of the Promised Land and the children of Israel, who are called the Jewish people today, according to terms the Holy One of Israel has made in this everlasting covenant. I will briefly explain how America's heritage facilitated great blessings and then in the 1990s, unlike ever before in its history, the USA officially chose the path, like the rest of the nations, to aggressively disregard the covenant land.

There are some little-known exciting events that shaped early American, and subsequent culture that still affect our lives today. While the Jewish people were having a miserable time under European persecution, much of it from the Catholic and Protestant church in the name of their own Messiah Jesus, something special happened in England. Winds of change began to blow in the 1500s that fanned a fire of philo-Semitism (the opposite of anti-Semitism) and this great love for the children of Israel captivated many in England! This was due to powerful moves of the Holy Spirit, which also caused great revivals of love for the Lord Jesus that took place in England.

While the rest of Europe was still in the throes of hating the Jewish people and experiencing the curses thereof, England was being raised up, by the One who blesses those who bless the Jewish people, to be the Empire of the world for hundreds of years! It was in this environment that the understanding of Bible prophecy was revealed to many in the United Kingdom and with it a desire to help the Jewish people return to their homeland. Hear the zealous words for the Lord of Hosts from His people in English pulpits and positions of government.

Charles H Spurgeon 1855 declared:

> I imagine it is impossible for you to read the Bible without seeing clearly there is an actual restoration of the children of Israel. Thither shall they go up; they shall come with weeping unto Zion that with supplications unto Jerusalem. May that happy day soon come! For when the Jews are restored then the fullness of the Gentiles shall be gathered in and as soon as they return then Jesus shall come upon Mount Zion to reign with His ancients gloriously! The day will yet come when the Jews who were the first apostles to the Gentiles-the first missionaries to us who were far off shall be gathered in again. Until that shall be, the fullness of the church's glory can never come! Matchless benefits to the world are bound up in the return of Israel. Their gathering in shall be as life from the dead. [1]

John and Charles Wesley were leaders of great English revivals who also founded the Methodist Church. They were also lovers of Israel who were caught up in the exciting things the Lord Jesus was doing in England. Charles Wesley wrote thousands of hymns and believed in sending the Jews back to their land of Israel which is an expression of Biblical Zionism.

Charles Wesley
Song from the Wesley's hymnal 1779:

O that the chosen band
Might now their brethren bring
And gathered out of every land
Present to Zion's King

Of all the ancient race
Not one be left behind
But each, impelled by secret grace
His way to Canaan find.

We know it must be done
For God hath spoke the word
All Israel shall their Savior own
To their first state restored
Rebuilt by His command
Jerusalem shall rise
Her temple on Moriah stand
Again and touch the skies

Send then thy servants forth
To call the Hebrews home
From east and west and south and north
Let all the wanderers come

Where'er in lands unknown
The fugitives remain
Bid every creature help them on
Thy holy mount to gain.[2]

British Foreign Secretary Lord Palmerston writes a letter to the British Ambassador in Constantinople.

August 11, 1840

There exists at present among the Jews dispersed over Europe a strong notion that the time is approaching when their nation is to return to Palestine. And consequently their wish to go thither has become more keen. And their thoughts are bent more intently than before upon the means of realizing that wish. Tis well known that the Jews of Europe possess great wealth. It would be of manifest importance to the Sultan to encourage the Jews to return to and settle in Palestine.[3]

The Balfour Declaration   November 2, 1917

During the First World War, British policy became gradually committed to the idea of establishing a Jewish home in Palestine (Eretz Yisrael). After discussions in the British Cabinet, and consultation with Zionist leaders, the decision was made known in the form of a letter by Arthur James Lord Balfour to Lord Rothschild. The letter represents the first political recognition of Zionist aims by a Great Power.[4]

Foreign Office   *November 2nd, 1917*

Dear Lord Rothschild,

I have much pleasure in conveying to you, on behalf of His Majesty's Government, the following declaration of sympathy with Jewish Zionist aspirations which has been submitted to, and approved by, the Cabinet.

"His Majesty's Government view with favour the establishment in Palestine of a national home for the Jewish people, and will use their best endeavours to facilitate the achievement of this object, it being clearly understood that nothing shall be done which may prejudice the civil and religious rights of existing non-Jewish communities in Palestine, or the rights and political status enjoyed by Jews in any other country."

*I should be grateful if you would bring this declaration to the knowl-
edge of the Zionist Federation.*

*Yours sincerely,
Arthur James Balfour*

Arthur James Balfour

Sadly, not long after the Balfour Declaration, England began to turn away from Israel to side with their Muslim neighbors in the oil business as the British developed a pan Arab oil strategy. Tragically for England, the Jewish aspirations stood as an obstacle to this lucrative relationship. In the same way the British Empire came up while they blessed Israel—it came crashing down as it cursed the covenant land and people. That land of Israel is in a covenant with the Holy One of Israel.

England proclaimed its policy toward the Promised Land in 1939 when the British White Paper became the official document announcing the United Kingdom was finished supporting the vision of Zionism. So much so that, as the British military occupied the land and seashore of Israel, they turned away the escaping Jews fleeing Nazi Europe to Israel (then Palestine) who were forced by the English to return to their tormentors and executioners. It was later that year the German Luftwaffe began to pound London from the air. England has never been the same and has lost its empire status.

In the same way England came up, America has also risen, as it has been a safe haven for the Jews and blessed by the Holy One of Israel. Here is a little known fact: there were Jews who were instrumental in the founding and fighting for the USA. After explaining how America through the early 1900s was a haven for the Jewish people, I will briefly list a few of many Jewish Americans who were prominent patriots.

Early America up through the 1800s was influenced greatly by England—especially in the area of faith in our Lord Jesus Christ. Some of the great men of faith, revivalists, and preachers like the Wesleys, Whitfield, Wilberforce, Spurgeon, George Mueller, and many others who loved the Jews and supported them returning to their homeland, also influenced American Christian Theology and society toward the Jewish people. There were also powerful similar revivals of love for the Lord Jesus and the Jewish people in America that spread here from England!

From that environment sprang up a love for the Jews in men like William Blackstone, D. L. Moody, and others who influenced American culture, including powerful statesmen and politicians. They worked together to create an atmosphere that culminated in a Baptist who became president of the United States and made the USA the first country to recognize the new State of Israel! President Harry Truman did so under great pressure, especially from the U.S. State Department, which had already turned against the Jews to not give American support for the new Israeli State.

Jewish American Patriots

In John McTernan's book, *As America Has Done to Israel,* he lists Jewish patriots who served America valiantly. Here are some of them:

- Haym Salomon—Significant financer of American Revolution without whom the war could not have been won.

- Uriah Levy—Commodore (equivalent of Admiral today) U.S. Navy 1792–1862, Restored Monticello (Jefferson's home)

"During the American Civil War, about nine thousand Jews fought for the North, and seven rose to the level of general."[5]

An Example of a Blessed Society

A small portion of George Washington's 1789 Letter To The Hebrew Congregations of Savannah Georgia:

> *May the same wonder-working Deity, who long since delivered the Hebrews from their Egyptian oppressors, planted them in a promised land, whose providential agency has lately been conspicuous in establishing these United States as an independent nation, still continue to water them with the dews of heaven and make the inhabitants of every denomination participate in the temporal and spiritual blessings of that people whose God is Jehovah.[6]*

William Blackstone was an evangelist and Zionist who wrote the Blackstone Memorial of 1891. He called for the nations to help bring the Jews, especially suffering in Russia, back to their homeland. Look at this abbreviated list of signers of the Blackstone Memorial:

- De Witt C Cregier, Mayor of Chicago
- Robert C. Davidson, Mayor of Baltimore
- Edwin H. Fitler, Mayor of Philadelphia
- Hugh J. Grant, Mayor of New York
- N. Matthews Jr., Mayor of Boston
- Wm. E. Russell, Governor of Massachusetts
- George Jones, *New York Times*
- Melville W. Fuller, Chief Justice of the US Supreme Court
- T. B. Reed, Speaker House Committee on Foreign Affairs
- William McKinley. Congressman, future president
- B. F. Jacobs, President, Security and Stock Exchange Commission
- Cyrus H. McCormick, President, McCormick Harvester *Company*[7]

American Presidents and the Land of Israel Today

In 1991 President George H. W. Bush began to make it official American policy to pressure Israel to give its covenant land away for the empty promise of peace and safety or security. The policy has been adopted by every American president since. This dangerous stance places Israel at a negotiating table with those who hate and want to kill them while they are coerced to give something away that Israel only jointly owns. The Land of Israel is in a covenant with two owners, the Jewish people and the Holy God of Israel. They cannot give something away that their God has commanded them to keep. And every nation that tries to make them give it away will be destroyed—that certainly is a curse!

> *"For behold, in those days and at that time, When I bring back the captives of Judah and Jerusalem, I will also gather all nations, And bring them down to the Valley of Jehoshaphat; And I will enter into judgment with them there On account of My people, My heritage Israel, Whom they have scattered among the nations; They have also divided up My land." (Joel 3:1–2)*

> *"For you yourselves know perfectly that the day of the Lord so comes as a thief in the night. For when they say, "Peace and safety!" then sudden destruction comes upon them, as labor pains upon a pregnant woman. And they shall not escape." (1 Thessalonians 5:2–3)*

These "Big Three" working together at the same time would create an environment that would spell certain disaster for the nation promoting them. It would not be a matter of "if" but "when," as the saying goes. The "when" is on the doorstep of today's America.

Chapter 6

America Today

. . . who exchanged the truth of God for the lie . . . (Romans 1:25)

*T*he early twentieth-century in America was a society much different from that of its founding. Of course there are many reasons—the one I believe most profound will be explained later. But there were a couple of landmark events worth mentioning, and then we can see America as it is today. We are moving toward the point of seeing what is going on in our nation from God's perspective—and the only hope He has left us that so few are discussing.

The Scopes Monkey Trial of 1925

The 1920s in America was a time of great "modernism." A collective outrage against Prohibition, teachings of Freud—who was a very strange cocaine addicted soul—and Darwin, the evolutionist, were prevalent game-changers among many including the modernists and so-called intellectuals.

The Scopes Monkey Trial was a circus-like legal event that stoked national attention by its entertaining yet profound courtroom drama that took place in a little town called Dayton, Tennessee. The three-ring event pitted famed William Jennings Bryan and his legal team, representing the prosecution and "Creation," and acclaimed trial attorney Clarence Darrow and his legal team representing a substitute teacher (John Scopes) being used as a pawn by an up-and-coming outfit called the American Civil Liberties Union—the ACLU. They were attempting to legalize teaching evolution in American schools. Though this trial did not directly accomplish their goal, it gave momentum for the later realization of their dream.

Supreme Court Decisions – Separation of Church and State

There were actually a series of legal cases that through time became Supreme Court rulings, which are commonly believed to be derived from the Constitution, and adhered to today under the umbrella term "Separation of Church And State." This term is nowhere to be found in the Constitution or any other founding American documents. It comes from an 1802 letter written by Thomas Jefferson to the Danbury Baptist Association in Connecticut. The letter pertains to protection against any Christian denomination's dominance over the other Christian sects in our society and the nation's governance. It had nothing to do with removing our Lord Jesus out of the public square due to atheists or those of other religions and their offense to the things of the God of the Bible.

As we look at America today let us compare the institutions and philosophies that govern and shape our society. Are their thoughts and ways comparable to those of our founders? Let's briefly peruse the landscape of government and positions of those who are in authority these days. You don't have to be a great scholar to see the difference.

We earlier heard a quote from the first president of the United States affirming the greatness of American education due to the foundation being laid by Jesus Christ. Certainly, the founders of this country believed it was a Christian nation. Yet, the current American president at the time of this writing and his last many predecessors, even if they took their oath of office on the Bible and professed to believe what is written on its pages, have by their words and actions demonstrated they are not the same kind of men. Quickly, here are some brief characterizations that show us these are men with a different spirit than that of America's founders.

President JFK: Many reported him as a chronic adulterer. And his escapades have become more widely known as his mistresses' accounts have been published and broadcasted.

President LBJ: Well-known for using horrible profanity and damning God's holy name along with many other very questionable things surrounding his presidency.

President Nixon: Watergate and its cover up.

President Gerald Ford: Along with most of these other Presidents listed—President Ford was a member of some very questionable organizations and secret societies:

"Gerald R. Ford, 1974–1977 R Bohemian Club, The Bilderberg Group, honorary Mason of the DeMolay-Legion of Honor, Council on Foreign Relations."[1]

President Jimmy Carter: Habitually sides with Israel's enemies. Mr. Carter advocates legitimizing terrorist groups as he is generally an Israel hater—aggressively mocks many of the things found in the Bible.

President Ronald Reagan: Thankfully, a breath of fresh air in many ways. Spoke openly of the Lord Jesus and the born-again faith, but also sadly has mixed reviews regarding Israel and the Jews. He fully embraced giving the covenant land away to Egypt packaged in the "Camp David Accords" in fulfillment of Jimmy Carter's "peace initiatives." This is all unraveling as Egypt is now ruled by radical Islam.

President George H. W. Bush: First American president to call for Israel to give covenant land of Israel to blatant Islamic Terrorists (Land for Peace).[2] Cabinet members who were very anti-Israel.

President William J. Clinton: Legally convicted and publicly admitted adulterer and perjurer, many questionable unanswered issues, sided often against Israel with terrorist Yasser Arafat.

President George W. Bush: Publicly often proclaimed that he was the first American president to officially present a plan to divide the covenant land of Israel calling for a Palestinian state in Jerusalem, Judea, and Samaria. This plan was the Saudi plan with an American name—Road Map to Peace. This president had close ties to the Saudi royal family due to oil interests. President Bush also was quoted as telling the world that Islam's god is the same as the God of the Bible.[3]

President Barack Hussein Obama: Promotes wholesale abortion, homosexual marriage, and the entire homosexual agenda in the name of Jesus Christ.

> *NOW, THEREFORE, I, BARACK OBAMA, President of the United States of America, by virtue of the authority vested in me by the Constitution and the laws of the United States, do hereby proclaim June 2012 as Lesbian, Gay, Bisexual, and Transgender Pride Month. I call upon the people of the United States to eliminate prejudice everywhere it exists, and to celebrate the great diversity of the American people.*
>
> *IN WITNESS WHEREOF, I have hereunto set my hand this first day of June,* **in the year of our Lord** *two thousand twelve, and of the Independence of the United States of America the two hundred and thirty-sixth.*[4]

President Obama also aggressively promotes giving the covenant land of Israel to Islam calling for Israel's return to 1967, or as some American military strategists call them, Auschwitz borders.

I am certainly the first one who should have been hit with stones for my sin, and have prayed for our presidents upon understanding our responsibility to do so as followers of the Lord Jesus. The reason I have cited the behavior of our country's modern leaders is to demonstrate, along with the other barometers of our society, that other than the name, America today does not resemble the nation that was founded upon faithfulness to the LORD!

Congress

Again, the old saying "those who live in glass houses should not throw stones" comes to mind while preparing to make a brief statement about our modern-day Congress. Before receiving Jesus Christ as Lord, I was a drug addict and have a very checkered past from it. It really is amazing grace that saved a wretch like me! I also did not know in my early years of following our Lord Jesus how to manage finances properly and learned some hard lessons that I will never forget about debt. But here are the two things I am doing: I have learned and teach people what not to do as well as what to do.

Having said that, you can go to any Internet search engine and learn that our modern-day Congress is full of people with criminal records, bankruptcies, and other really bad behavior. The problem is that from the way they are leading this country, it is obvious that many have not yet learned from their past mistakes. If that is true, our country, to a great degree, is being led by people with a criminal mind who also apparently do not yet understand the fatal results of unbridled debt to a nation's finances.

American Schools

In the summer of 1962, the year this author was born, prayer was officially taken out of school due to the brilliant church and state decisions by the black robes in D.C. If you do a little research, you will find that the crime rates across the board and pregnancy-out-of-wedlock rates began to spike and then skyrocket. They have not returned to anywhere near what they were before as the absence of our Creator in schools has made a breeding ground for lawlessness. The expressions in our society of rejection of the Lord Jesus Christ, upon whose principles this country was founded, laid out the welcome mat for the drug, sex, false gods, and hatred of the true God craze that quickly rushed in and replaced Him and His protective boundaries.

Evolution

After the "Monkey Trial" evolution began to spread like wild fire through the American schools. Today of course in most of them it is illegal to teach "Biblical Creation" as the way man came into being. So, the likes of Mr. Darwin and his disciples have had their day in the sun through the American School system. And what has it "created"? Today, in the highest percentages ever in this land's history, our society believes that man was not created by God in His image. No, they tell us we have evolved, from not much more than thin air, to higher life forms, through "survival of the fittest," then to monkeys—to people who live today. Please forgive me for skipping some of the steps to our grossly misperceived ascension.

Close to the time of this writing, only forty percent of Americans believe we were created by God, while about thirty-nine percent believe in evolution, and is it any wonder the rest just don't know what to believe? Think of this: about four out of ten in America believe that we evolved from basically nothing and therefore the Bible is not true regarding our creation, and more importantly—is untrue about our Creator![5]

Atheism and Higher Learning

In many of the schools that were founded as seminaries and Bible colleges, the thinking of the faculty and students today are certainly poles apart from their founders. These schools that were once bastions of belief in the cause of Christ have been taken over by people greatly opposed to and even avowed enemies of those beliefs. Today's institutions are the last thing these men would have ever envisioned, and if there is anything of which the founders would have said, "Please—whatever you do, don't let this happen!" that is exactly what has happened!

Atheism and a condescending hatred for the things of God have become the norm at these and most other of the nation's public colleges. And let's face it—they come out of the political system called "left," "liberal," or "progressive." That is not to say that all liberals are atheists or God haters, but many of their political camp certainly are. Those who are so vehemently against the God of the Bible in today's America are also the so called" liberal, progressive, left." Here are telling articles explaining the imbalances in places of higher learning in today's America:

So, for example, at Cornell, of the 172 faculty members whose party affiliation was recorded, 166 were liberal (Democrats or Greens) and six were conservative (Republicans or Libertarians). At Stanford the liberal-conservative ratio was 151–17. At San Diego State it was 80–11. At SUNY Binghamton, 35–1. At UCLA, 141–9. At the University of Colorado-Boulder, 116–5. Reflecting on these gross disparities, The American Enterprise's editor, Karl Zinsmeister, remarked: "Today's colleges and universities . . . do not, when it comes to political and cultural ideas, look like America.

At about the same time, a poll of Ivy League professors commissioned by the Center for the Study of Popular Culture found that more than 80 percent of those who voted in 2000 had cast their ballots for Democrat Al Gore while just 9 percent backed Republican George W. Bush. While 64 percent said they were "liberal" or "somewhat liberal," only 6 percent described themselves as "somewhat conservative"—and none at all as "conservative."[6]

So, if those who are atheists and even God-hating professors get hold of youth who don't believe in the Lord Jesus or are not sure that He exists, they have a free hand, and four to seven, eight, or more years, to mold the students into the likeness of themselves. Listen to the word of the Lord about these "free thinkers":

*"And even as they did not like to retain God in their knowledge, God gave them over to a debased mind, to do those things which are not fitting; being filled with all unrighteousness, sexual immorality, wickedness, covetousness, maliciousness; full of envy, murder, strife, deceit, evil-mindedness; they are whisperers, backbiters, **haters of God** . . ." (Romans 1:28–30, emphasis added)*

False Religions

When the founders of America pursued freedom of religion and penned their names to the US Constitution and Bill of Rights they had no imagination to think they were protecting the worship of false gods across America in such a way that it would threaten the very principles upon which this nation was founded—-the Word of God! All you have to do is read their writings, some found in this book and elsewhere, to understand this important fact. Of course, the "free thinkers" mentioned above, who are at war with the true and living God, love to support the cause of all that is against Him.

So, now due to the sensitivities of atheists and the adherents of the false gods and religions, it would be offensive to have the Ten Commandments on American courtroom walls, or crosses on government property, and of course any representation of the Lord Jesus at functions like school football games, graduation events, and so on would also be off limits. Does anyone remember the first of the Ten Commandments— "You shall have no other gods before Me" (Exodus 20:3)—meaning before My eyes? How offensive to the true and living Giver of the American inalienable rights. Folks, men cannot take those rights away, but the Lord Jesus can.

We should protect everyone's right to worship equally, but not at the expense of declaring war on the God Who has never lost a fight—Almighty Yahweh (The LORD)!

"The LORD *is* a man of war; The LORD *is* His name." (Exodus 15:3)

Abortion as It Relates to Early America

Can you imagine George Washington signing a bill or Chief Justice John Jay mentioned earlier making judgments that would legalize killing babies in their mother's womb to protect the rights of the mothers who choose to kill their unborn children?

I can hear them now "My fellow Americans, since our society is one of pleasures such as fornication, drunkenness, and wanton debauchery, we need to preserve the capacity for our citizens to act as wickedly as they like, and not punish them with an unwanted child. So heretofore, we endorse the legalizing of killing the unwanted babies and thus preserving the rights of their freedom-loving parents."

I say this with great sadness: how barbaric and sick our society has become. Here is the word of the Lord about the matter:

"You shall not afflict any widow or fatherless child. If you afflict them in any way, and they cry at all to Me, I will surely hear their cry; and My wrath will become hot, and I will kill you with the

sword; your wives shall be widows, and your children father-less." (Exodus 22:22–24)

I would suppose that the LORD considers the killing of over fifty-five million babies in the womb, in America alone, since the early 1970s and the Roe v Wade decision by the men in black, to constitute the affliction of fatherless children. I must also state clearly that vengeance is the LORD's and I advocate taking every and ONLY non-violent measures to spare these babies. The terrible judgment for the innocent blood of so many babies is going to be devastating on this country.

Homosexuality as a Civil Right?

The homosexual—politically correct, sacred cow fascist move-ment has very effectively promoted deviant sexual behavior to the status of the civil rights protection legitimately given to provide equal rights for those of every ethnicity. It is a politically correct and fascist movement because as far as those who promote this fool-ishness your First Amendment rights under the U.S. Constitution to free speech are thrown under the bus if you call the homosexual lifestyle and behavior what it is—WRONG AND SINFUL! It is fascist because of the aggressive attempt to marginalize and demonize people who stand up for the truth in love, which threatens their movement. Once a society accepts this kind of marginalizing move-ment, the next steps can be very dangerous—just look at Germany and Italy in the 1940s and Rwanda in the 1990s.

Just ask Mr. Dan Cathy of Chick-fil-A who spoke in a radio inter-view of the judgment of God found in the Bible for those who would change marriage to accommodate the homosexual move-ment. Upon hearing his statement mayors and city officials in Chi-cago, Boston, and other cities disgracefully attacked him and his company refreshingly built upon Biblical principles. Oh, do you even recognize this country?

So now our children, taught by the National Education Associa-tion (NEA), are being fed this movement's lies and darkness and learn its ways instead of the Lord's. It is the same way in businesses as most of the Fortune 500 companies have sexual orientation training or rules supporting this wicked movement. And the military and local governments across the country are being polluted with this strange deluge. It is getting this way across the spectrum of society—the BIBLE IS OFFICIALLY OUT AND HOMOSEXUALITY IS OFFICIALLY IN!

Bibles? Nah . . . "Gay pride"? Yep!

> "The Chaplain Alliance for Religious Liberty says it's a sad state of affairs when the U.S. military decides Bibles are out but "gay pride" is in."[7]

Corporations urge Supreme Court to embrace gay marriage

> "More than 200 businesses on Wednesday urged the U.S. Supreme Court to strike down a federal law that restricts the definition of marriage to heterosexual unions, in one of corporate America's most prominent efforts to support same-sex marriage."[8]

> "For this reason God gave them up to vile passions. For even their women exchanged the natural use for what is against nature. Likewise also the men, leaving the natural use of the woman, burned in their lust for one another, men with men committing what is shameful, and receiving in themselves the penalty of their error which was due." (Romans 1:26–27)

Again, the important reminder with this verse and others regarding this sin is that God is the one who judges, as followers of Jesus Christ we are to tell the truth and warn all people in LOVE!

First Ever Gay Pride Event at Pentagon Features Messages from President and Defense Secretary—on Video[9]

At West Point Military Academy two women actually married each other! Oh Lord Jesus, save us from ourselves. Can you imagine such things in America?

So, here is the question: Has America sinned against the Lord Jesus with persistent unfaithfulness? The Bible is clear about what our nation has become. It is persistently sinful (full of sin). Now, we will see in chapters to come what the Lord Jesus is unfolding for America and for those who will go to His place of refuge, *America's Ark.*

Chapter 7

A Persistently Unfaithful Nation

The word of the LORD came again to me, saying: "Son of man, when a land sins against Me by persistent unfaithfulness . . . (Ezekiel 14:12–13)

*A*ll my life I have loved the United States of America. There is an old saying out there that compares being born in America to many other places on the earth. I think this says it all:

"Being born in America is like starting off on third base." For those reading who have never watched a baseball game, this means that being born in America gives a person an incredibly big head start in life. Having travelled extensively to third world countries, I know this to be true in many ways in my own life and I am thankful to have been born and raised in the USA!

Similarly, I cannot imagine the Prophet Jeremiah would have wished to be anything but an Israeli. I am confident that he loved his heritage and cherished Israel. Crushed over Israel's judgment for sin he said this:

"Oh, that my head were waters, And my eyes a fountain of tears, That I might weep day and night For the slain of the daughter of my people!" (Jeremiah 9:1)

Jeremiah was not a casual citizen of Israel, but sowed his life into loving God and country—a true patriot! The trouble he endured for that love can only be realized by prayerfully reading the entire book of Jeremiah. However, when he warned of the coming judgment from the LORD he was despised by his countrymen:

"And when he was in the Gate of Benjamin, a captain of the guard was there whose name was Irijah the son of Shelemiah, the son of Hananiah; and he seized Jeremiah the prophet, saying, "You are defecting to the Chaldeans!" (Jeremiah 37:13)

Jeremiah was simply warning the people from the mouth of the Lord that He was raising up Babylon to judge His people unless they repent. When the people of Judah refused to turn from their wickedness, the Lord told them through Jeremiah that God was turning Israel and the surrounding nations over to King Nebuchadnezzar of Babylon. He also warned them not to resist the Babylonian Ruler. And for this difficult obedience to the God of Israel Jeremiah was seen as a traitor. This weeping prophet gave them words of life and the way to live and prosper through the judgment, but they refused to listen. You see, Jeremiah still loved God and country. There is no more patriotic act than to tell our countrymen, "Thus says the Lord!"

With this perspective in view, we need to hear today from the Lord and listen when His prophets speak. We have been reminded by our brief walk through American history of its godly heritage, again not perfect and with many historical sins, yet a foundation of Biblical faithfulness to the Lord. We have also observed that after all the opportunities to maintain a faithful nation, and even grow in God's grace as a more faithful land, that America has become persistently entrenched in aggressive sins against the God of the Bible. Here is the inescapable and difficult-to-face reality: America clearly is exactly what was being described by Ezekiel in terms of a persistently unfaithful land.

And due to this category of sin, in which we as Americans find our land immersed, we should look at the scriptures and ask a question: Does Ezekiel have something here for us to understand and apply in this hour? Let's look at the first warning that leads up to the four judgments:

> *"The word of the LORD came again to me, saying: "Son of man, when a land sins against Me by persistent unfaithfulness, I will stretch out My hand against it . . ." (Ezekiel 14:12–13)*

I have a very important question that will really define whether you can believe, or not, what the Lord is doing today with America. Please listen to the question, answer it from your current understanding, and then please listen to God's word—the Bible. Here it is:

In judgment does the Lord only allow calamity, or does He also cause it?

The prevailing thoughts of most believers I have talked to through the years range from "the devil causes calamity when it strikes in America" to "God allows it." This is what is most often taught from pulpits and is therefore most often believed by Christians. But is that what the Bible teaches? At this critical hour let's see what God's word says and believe it!

In the Ezekiel 14 passage does the prophet tell us that the Lord will allow judgment or cause it? Ezekiel clearly warns that the Lord is stretching out His hand of judgment upon that sinful land. But let's not form a doctrine from just one passage of scripture. We know the Bible best interprets the Bible. So, let's look at other passages to learn the truth.

We can first look at the nation of Israel. One important distinction is that the Lord is in a covenant with Israel. He is not in a covenant with America. Actually, there are many examples of how He deals with Israel that will be very appropriate as we later look at the American Christians. But for now, let's look at Israel as a land and country and then other Gentile empires.

> *"I form the light and create darkness, I make peace and create calamity; I, the LORD, do all these things." (Isaiah 45:7)*

"If a trumpet is blown in a city, will not the people be afraid? If there is calamity in a city, will not the LORD have done it?" (Amos 3:6)

Though strange according to most Americans' Christian understanding, in the Bible where the Lord is judging, He claims direct responsibility for the trouble. In the above Isaiah passage the Lord takes responsibility for calamity. In like manner the Lord takes direct credit for calamity in the Amos verse as well.

With regard to who gives life and takes it away, does man have the final decision who lives and who dies? King Saul, the first king of Israel, had horribly turned away from the Holy One of Israel. He and some of his men were in a fierce battle, and King Saul was killed.

Then the Philistines followed hard after Saul and his sons. And the Philistines killed Jonathan, Abinadab, and Malchishua, Saul's sons. The battle became fierce against Saul. The archers hit him, and he was severely wounded by the archers. Then Saul said to his armor bearer, "Draw your sword, and thrust me through with it, lest these uncircumcised men come and thrust me through and abuse me." But his armor bearer would not, for he was greatly afraid. Therefore Saul took a sword and fell on it. (1 Samuel 31:2–4)

So, here is my question: Who killed King Saul? Was it the Philistines? Was it Saul himself? The answer may surprise you—the Bible clearly answers the question for us:

"So Saul died for his unfaithfulness which he had committed against the LORD, because he did not keep the word of the LORD, and also because he consulted a medium for guidance. But he did not inquire of the LORD; therefore He killed him, and turned the kingdom over to David the son of Jesse." (1 Chronicles 10:13–14)

Our Bibles tell us that The Lord killed Saul for his unfaithfulness that he had committed against the Holy One of Israel. Ultimately, it isn't the Philistines or even Saul who took his own life, but what we see here is that the Sovereign Holy One of Israel does what He wants to do with whom He wants to do it and uses all His creation to do so! The Lord killed Saul for his unfaithfulness—what is Ezekiel talking about in the passage atop this chapter?

In case that is not enough Biblical evidence here is a passage that puts it plainly regarding who has power over life and death:

> *"Now see that I, even I, am He, And there is no God besides Me; I kill and I make alive; I wound and I heal; Nor is there any who can deliver from My hand." (Deuteronomy 32:39)*

Gentile Empires

When empires like the Babylonian, Persian, Greek, and Roman powers would rise and fall how did that happen? How do they rise and fall today? Is it due to the next super power coming up and decimating the other by its own greatness? Well, no not really. Again, what do our Bibles say?

Jeremiah was a great prophet who had much to say about the world in which we live today and in the future. Sadly, we live in an evangelical Christian environment that by and large has not learned the prophets. Their words are being fulfilled all around us in "living color"! The Bible teaches that Jeremiah was called by the Lord to be a prophet to the Gentiles or nations.

> *"Before I formed you in the womb I knew you; Before you were born I sanctified you; I ordained you a prophet to the nations." (Jeremiah 1:5)*

> *"See, I have this day set you over the nations and over the kingdoms, To root out and to pull down, To destroy and to throw down, To build and to plant." (Jeremiah 1:10)*

Jeremiah speaks here of the Lord's prophetic words pulling down and raising up empires! He would do so based on their repentance or lack thereof. If they would not repent it was the hand of the Lord our God who would bring down empires.

> *The instant I speak concerning a nation and concerning a kingdom, to pluck up, to pull down, and to destroy it, if that nation against whom I have spoken turns from its evil, I will relent of the disaster that I thought to bring upon it. And the instant I speak concerning a nation and concerning a kingdom, to build and to plant it, if it does evil in My sight so that it does not obey My voice, then I will relent concerning the good with which I said I would benefit it. (Jeremiah 18:7–10)*

The lyrics of the traditional American spiritual are still true: "He's got the whole world in His hands"! And though He may use different means and tools in His creation—people, places, and things—ultimately the Lord Jesus is the One doing the blessing and raising up and also responsible for the judgment and calamity.

There are some who would resort to saying "Ah but these are Old Testament ways of the Lord, He doesn't operate that way anymore." The Bible tells us in the New Testament that "all scripture is God breathed" (2 Timothy 3:16). And there are other New Testament passages that show us the error of not listening to the prophets, of which I will list a few. But to quickly settle the matter I would simply remind us of the judgments found through the book of Revelation in the New Testament.

The Lord's judgment upon Ananias for lying to the Holy Spirit:

> *"Then Ananias, hearing these words, fell down and breathed his last. So great fear came upon all those who heard these things." (Acts 5:5)*

> *"For whatever things were written before were written for our learning, that we through the patience and comfort of the Scriptures might have hope." (Romans 15:4)*

> *"Jesus Christ is the same yesterday, today, and forever." (Hebrews 13:8)*

Having looked at this Biblical evidence, clearly demonstrating that the Lord sends calamity in judgment, I have some more questions: Do we see clearly all around us the four judgments of the Lord described by Ezekiel beginning to be poured out on this land called America? Like an approaching hurricane's outer bands of wind and rain, do we see the storm coming in quickly? If so, thankfully we can earnestly learn the way to survive the catastrophe that is upon us in what I call *America's Ark.* This author strongly believes the Lord gave Ezekiel the only hopeful way forward for the people of America, and the world, who would listen to Him. Let's begin by taking an honest look at the judgments.

Chapter 8

Famine

. . . I will break the staff of the bread thereof . . . (Ezekiel 14:13 KJV)

*T*he first of the four judgments listed in Ezekiel that are falling upon America is—can you believe it—famine. America for many years has not only had more opportunities to feed itself than most in the world can imagine, but it has also been the bread basket for the world! Often when I have travelled to Africa I have seen USAID bags full of wheat and other products from America given to help the populations of hungry countries. In most of America's history we have enjoyed the great blessing of abundance as it relates to food, and suffered little with the one billion hungry people on earth today.

However, when the Lord says that He will *"cut off its supply of bread"* or *"break the staff of the bread thereof"* (KJV) think of the Hebrew Old Testament definitions of what He will do to the food supply: *break in pieces, wreck, crush, rupture, cripple, shatter, ruin.* Let's look at the entire passage as it relates to famine.

> *"The word of the LORD came again to me, saying: "Son of man, when a land sins against Me by persistent unfaithfulness, I will stretch out My hand against it; I will cut off its supply of bread, send famine on it, and cut off man and beast from it."* *(Ezekiel 14:12–13)*

What the Lord is saying through His prophet is that when the Holy One of Israel stretches out His hand in judgment to cause famine that people and animals will die from starvation. The devastation to the food supply will be severe and comprehensive. And there will be no way to stop it—there will only be refuge in the *Ark,* or place of provision, He designates.

We certainly will look at this safe haven very closely and having this information I pray you will decide to go in and receive the umbrella of protection. Many will try to store up food, yet if they have not fled to *America's Ark* it will not matter—it will not be enough, or someone will take it, or some other tragic scenario, but only the way our Lord Jesus has provided will protect us from His hand of judgment on the food supply.

Father God, Not Mother Nature

There was a man in our church years ago who was trying to convince me that it was okay to use the term Mother Nature describing weather-related issues. Oh friends, Mother Nature is a term describing a Babylonian pagan goddess—it has no place in our vocabulary as followers of our Lord Jesus. You see, there is no Mother Nature, but there most assuredly is the Father God! And God the Son—the Son of God still is the one who the wind and the waves obey! So, unless your Jesus is not the One who controls the wind and the waves we know that weather patterns which determine so much of our environment, and our very lives, are from the Lord.

> *So the men marveled, saying, "Who can this be, that even the winds and the sea obey Him?" (Matthew 8:27)*

> *"You broke open the fountain and the flood; You dried up mighty rivers. The day is Yours, the night also is Yours; You have prepared the light and the sun." (Psalm 74:15–16)*

Did the Lord use such things to judge people in the Bible? If so, has He stopped doing that in our generation for some reason? Or could it be that He only does that with others—not Americans? Since weather is so significant to food stores, let's look at the Good Book to see what part it played in the lives of people in the Bible when the Lord would stretch out His hand to judge.

Rain and Floods

Of course the rain and flood in Noah's day is the greatest example of how the Lord uses this means to judge the earth and its inhabitants. He promised to not destroy the entire earth with rainstorm and flood ever again (Genesis 9:11). But, He did not promise to refrain from judging regions this way. Let's look further and determine if He continued to use rain and flood to regionally judge people and their lands. Incidentally, a tempest in the Bible is defined this way: rain-shower, thunderstorm, flood of rain, downpour, rainstorm.

> *"Therefore thus says the Lord GOD: 'I will cause a stormy wind to break forth in My fury; and there shall be a flooding rain in My anger, and great hailstones in fury to consume it.'" (Ezekiel 13:13)*

> *"You will be punished by the LORD of hosts With thunder and earthquake and great noise, With storm and tempest And the flame of devouring fire." (Isaiah 29:6)*

> *"The LORD will cause His glorious voice to be heard, And show the descent of His arm, With the indignation of His anger And the flame of a devouring fire, With scattering, tempest, and hailstones." (Isaiah 30:30)*

Drought and Fire

We see in these verses that along with rain, flooding, earthquakes, and other disasters that drought and fire, caused by withholding rain, is also part of the judgment when the Lord is dealing with the land of the rebellious. Here are more passages addressing God's ways regarding withholding rain.

"Therefore the showers have been withheld, And there has been no latter rain. You have had a harlot's forehead; You refuse to be ashamed." (Harlots would wear a special head bandanna or other markings to designate their trade.) (Jeremiah 3:3)

". . . lest the LORD's anger be aroused against you, and He shut up the heavens so that there be no rain, and the land yield no produce, and you perish quickly from the good land which the LORD is giving you." (Deuteronomy 11:17)

"When the heavens are shut up and there is no rain because they have sinned against You, when they pray toward this place and confess Your name, and turn from their sin because You afflict them . . ." (1 Kings 8:35)

Elijah is sent by the Lord to tell wicked King Ahab of the curse on the land:

"And Elijah the Tishbite, of the inhabitants of Gilead, said to Ahab, 'As the LORD God of Israel lives, before whom I stand, there shall not be dew nor rain these years, except at my word.'" (1 Kings 17:1)

"I also withheld rain from you, When there were still three months to the harvest. I made it rain on one city, I withheld rain from another city. One part was rained upon, And where it did not rain the part withered. So two or three cities wandered to another city to drink water, But they were not satisfied; Yet you have not returned to Me," Says the LORD. (Amos 4:7–8)

"Therefore, as the fire devours the stubble, And the flame consumes the chaff, So their root will be as rottenness, And their blossom will ascend like dust; Because they have rejected the law of the LORD of hosts . . . " (Isaiah 5:24)

"Are there any among the idols of the nations that can cause rain? Or can the heavens give showers? Are You not He, O LORD

our God? Therefore we will wait for You, Since You have made all these." (Jeremiah 14:22)*

And there are many more examples through the Bible of how the Lord of Hosts literally ruins the food supply in the land that sins against Him with persistent unfaithfulness. That being established let's consider our beloved USA and how it has been sorely affected by the hand of the Lord in the last two decades—1990s and beyond to the time of this writing in late 2012 and beginning 2013. And let's consider how that relates to the "Big Three."

In 1991 the proverbial straw that broke the camel's back dropped onto the camel in the USA. It was then that President George H. W. Bush began the terrible American policy to throw Israel under the bus at the Madrid Peace Conference. This was the beginning of the end for America. It was here that official U.S. policy demanded that Israel give the covenant land away for peace. It was also here that the most terrifying acts of God began to be poured out on America.

The strange and mystifying storm made into a movie called the Perfect Storm, Andrew in Florida, and other Florida storms that redefined the Sunshine State as "Hurricane Alley," were just the beginning of the new normal for America. Hurricanes in number and severity spiked until a major American city was so devastated that parts of it remain unrepaired to this day—Katrina in New Orleans. And of course Hurricane Sandy, with estimated cost of $100 billion dollars, has devastated part of Northeast America.

There are books like *As America Has Done To Israel* by Chaplain John McTernan, mentioned earlier, that chronicle how the same day of wicked behavior or events pertaining to abortion, homosexuality, and pressing Israel, that these storms would eerily hit the USA. One of these nasty tempests went right over my house in Pearland, Texas—Hurricane Ike in 2008.

Of course, there have also been terrible record breaking killer tornado clusters and other floods and rainstorms. It is not that people disbelieve these things are happening like never before. It is that they try to blame the horrendous changes all around us on everything else except our horrible national sins and the Lords's judgment upon them. Remember, insurance companies up until not that long ago would call these things ACTS OF GOD! Now they are attributed as being from everything else but God. Be sure of this— God will not be mocked, and He will receive glory!

So, due to the judgments of Father God not Mother Nature— heavy rain, flooding, hurricanes, and the absence of rain causing droughts and record smashing fires, the farm lands and crops across America are being ruined just like the Lord warned—and most Americans refuse to listen. At the time of writing this book historical drought and fires are consuming hundreds of thousands of acres in many states in America. During this disastrous crop failure news outlets are proclaiming the trouble Americans are just beginning to experience with little clue where this is all headed.

NEWS ARTICLES

Midwest drought worsens, food inflation to rise[1] -Reuters
Wed., Jul 25 2012

Brutal July heat a new U.S. record[2] —*CNN.com*
July 2012 was the hottest month on record for contiguous United States since recordkeeping began in 1895, according to NOAA.

Drought's impact on food prices could worsen hunger in America[3]—
Yahoo.com

Hummingbirds, facing drought and food shortage, get some human help[4]—*CBSnews.com*

Cows eating candy during the drought[5]—*WPRI.com*
Ranchers have struggled with skyrocketing corn prices, because the drought has made feeding their livestock very expensive. But one rancher has turned to a very sweet solution.

At Mayfield's United Livestock Commodities, owner Joseph Watson is tweaking the recipe for success. "Just to be able to sur-vive, we have to look for other sources of nutrition," he said. His 1,400 cattle are no longer feeding off corn. The prices, Watson says, are too high to keep corn in stock. So earlier this year, he began to buy second-hand candy.

Food shortages could force world into vegetarianism, warn scientists: Water scarcity effect on food production means radical steps will be needed to feed population expected to reach 9bn by 2050[6]—The Guardian-UK
Record-breaking wildfire season could get worse in Texas[7]—The Associated Press
Record breaking heat as Colorado fires rage across the state[8]—Examiner.com
Wyoming Wildfire Grows As Montana And Colorado Fires Continue To Burn[9]—Huffingtonpost.com

The drought deepens, the fires rage, the crops die, and even the Mighty Mississippi River is drying up hindering the barges that are carrying the fewer harvested crops from making their journey to markets. USA energy policy has much of its corn being made into gasoline while the corn is becoming less available and more expensive. A report came out recently that explained that seventy-five

Grounded barges on Mississippi River

percent of goods bought in most American supermarkets contain corn—fewer goods and higher prices will be the result.

Imagine a society like America today—certainly not like the one that stood in line for bread during the Great Depression. No, when this violent, prideful, arrogant, sense of entitlement society gets hungry—WATCH OUT! The incredible sparks that are about to fly are unimaginable. And according to the God of the Bible it is coming sure and certain. Americans are going to learn something about which they have known little—HUNGER.

Interestingly, when we think of the judgment on Sodom and Gomorrah we think first of homosexuality. But the Bible teaches that something happened to Sodom to cause the Lord to turn them over to a dark heart that would produce such an evil society long before they became infested with homosexuality. Once again through the prophetic words of Ezekiel we find that the Lord compares Israel in its sin to Sodom, and there we find the conditions of Sodom that led to such depravity:

> *"Look, this was the iniquity of your sister Sodom: She and her daughter had pride, fullness of food, and abundance of idleness; neither did she strengthen the hand of the poor and needy. And they were haughty and committed abomination before Me; therefore I took them away as I saw fit." (Ezekiel 16:49–50)*

In the midst of these variables that make this very dangerous equation, which tragically describes America to the letter, is something that we see the Lord dealing with in America's generation of judgment—*fullness of food*. Yet even in the midst of coming terrible famine the hands of the Lord are extended for mercy in America's Ark! Don't forget—there is good news ahead.

Chapter 9

The Call of the Wild

"If I cause wild beasts to pass through the land . . ." (Ezekiel 14:15)

As modern Americans, in some areas we have so little under-standing of the ways of the "Ancient of Days" our Father in Heaven and the timeless Son of God (Daniel 7:13). It is as if we have an American Jesus who simply doesn't operate like the Holy One of Israel. He operates according to American ways and does things that we understand in the way that makes sense to us. But the true and living Jesus Christ operates by His own ways. And one of the things He tells us in the Bible is that the animal kingdom is part of His Kingdom:

> *"I know all the fowls of the mountains: and the wild beasts of the field are mine." (Psalm 50:11, KJV)*

In Genesis after the great flood the Lord gave animals a fear of man. Noah and his righteous family experienced the greatest dominion over animals ever documented from the time after sin came into the earth through Adam (Romans 5:12). There have always been exceptions to this, but generally wild animals have a God-given fear of man that makes them more afraid of us than we are of them. Some of the most ferocious animals on the planet have historically been very afraid of mankind.

"And the fear of you and the dread of you shall be on every beast of the earth, on every bird of the air, on all that move on the earth, and on all the fish of the sea. They are given into your hand." (Genesis 9:2)

However, as this generation of Americans, and the whole world, quickly becomes more like Noah's wicked society before the flood, the fear of man which the Lord gave animals is being removed. And in God's word we can see how the Lord used animals to judge rebellious societies. Here are some examples of this in scripture:

As the people of the Lord rebelled against Him:

"I will also send wild beasts among you, which shall rob you of your children, and destroy your cattle, and make you few in number; and your high ways shall be desolate." (Leviticus 26:22)

Regarding the enemies of Israel:

"And I will send hornets before you, which shall drive out the Hivite, the Canaanite, and the Hittite from before you." (Exodus 23:28)

As they mocked the prophet of the Lord:

"So he turned around and looked at them, and pronounced a curse on them in the name of the LORD. And two female bears came out of the woods and mauled forty-two of the youths." (2 Kings 2:24)

Deliverance from wild beasts for those walking under the blessings and protection of the Lord:

"And I will make with them a covenant of peace, and will cause the evil beasts to cease out of the land: and they shall dwell safely in the wilderness, and sleep in the woods." (Ezekiel 34:25)

This brings us back to Ezekiel and his prophecy for the sinfully, persistently, unfaithful land.

In all of these passages the Lord dealt with people according to their respect of Him and His ways. For those who instigated His wrath, along with the others in the orchestra of His judgment, He includes the animal section to play their part with great precision. So it is today in the sinfully, persistently, unfaithful land of America.

"If I cause wild beasts to pass through the land . . . and they empty it, and make it so desolate that no man may pass through because of the beasts . . ." (Ezekiel 14:15)

I am watching more strange and unusual circumstances every day in America—many including injury and deaths caused by wild animals. It is getting stranger by the moment! These are things that we simply did not see with this kind of frequency and, for lack of a better word, weirdness. I am going to list some news headlines that certainly got my attention. And realize this: I am not listing the diseases that many creatures bring with them into the "unfaithful land" equation. In this chapter I am just dealing with the aggression from the animal kingdom toward man. Some of the diseases will be discussed in the fourth judgment given through Ezekiel.

Shark Attacks

I will never forget the time my dad took me to see the movie *Jaws* in the theatre when it came out in 1975. My usually very cool and collected father stood up and said an expletive the first time the shark's head came out of the water to threaten those hunting it. From that time sharks have been on the mind of Americans like never before in our history. That being said, the reality is that great white sharks are aggressively hunting closer to the shores in American waters and bull sharks have adapted to fresh water in ways that take them as far in American rivers as Missouri! If you do an Internet search you will find that bull sharks are found in places like Missouri and Illinois. Bull sharks are very aggressive and are considered by many as the most dangerous to humans.

The bull shark, Carcharhinus leucas, also known as the Zambezi shark (UK: Zambesi shark) or unofficially Zambi in Africa and Nicaragua shark in Nicaragua, is a shark commonly found worldwide in warm, shallow waters along coasts and in rivers. The bull shark is known for its aggressive nature, predilection for warm shallow water, and presence in brackish and freshwater systems including estuaries and rivers.

The bull shark can thrive in both saltwater and freshwater and can travel far up rivers. They have even been known to travel as far up as Indiana in the Ohio River, although there have been few recorded attacks. They are probably responsible for the majority of near-shore shark attacks, including many attacks attributed to other species. Bull sharks are not actually true freshwater sharks, despite their ability to survive in freshwater habitats (unlike the river sharks of the genus <u>Glyphis</u>).[1]-Big Fishes of the World.blogspot

Surfer, swimmer, shark! Attacks on the rise[2]–USA Today

Shark attacks rise, fishing tactics may be at fault[3]—limitedlands.com

Shark Attack in Cape Cod, They are saying possible Bull shark. . . . Shark sightings have been on the rise in the area, and great[4]—Foxnews.com

Sharks Populations Decreasing, Attacks on the Rise—Science[5]—Redorbit.com

Are Sharks More Likely to Attack in American Waters?[6]—livescience.com Statistically speaking, sharks in American waters are the most blood-thirsty of all their foreign counterparts, at least in respect to humans.

California surfer killed in shark attack[7]—CBS

Vandenberg Air Force Base, Calif.—A shark attack at an Air Force base beach has claimed the life of an experienced 39-year-old surfer, following months of frequent shark sightings along the central California coast. Francisco Javier Solorio Jr., of Orcutt, was bitten in his upper torso while he was surfing with a friend who witnessed the attack. They were in the ocean off the coastal Vandenberg Air Force Base, on Surf Beach in Lompoc, the Santa Barbara County sheriff's department said in a statement.

"His friend ended up swimming over and pulling him from the water where he received first aid," said sheriff's Sgt. Mark A. Williams. Solorio was pronounced dead at the scene…. Surf Beach, Lucas Ransom, a 19-year-old student at the University of California, Santa Barbara, died when a shark nearly severed his leg as he body-boarded.

Multiple sightings of great white sharks forces closure of Cape[8]—*NY Daily News*

A popular Cape Cod beach was closed to swimming over the Labor Day weekend after several great white sharks were spotted dangerously close . . .

Great white sharks: Close encounters on East and West coasts[9]—*csmonitor.com*

And Then There Are The Bears:

Black bears fight each other in front yard of Florida home[10]–*ksdk.com*

Fatal Black Bear Attacks on the Rise[11]—*discovery.com. Since 1960 in North America, more than 50 people were killed by black bears in the wild.*

Bear Attacks on the Rise in North and South Carolina[12]—*yahoo.com
    Beware of Bears in Your Area*

Bear Attacks in Central New Hampshire on the Rise [13]—*yahoo.com*

Deadly Bear Attacks Could Rise[14]—*ABC News*

Are Hungry Bears in Yellowstone Attacking Humans for Food?[15]—*outsideonline.com
    For 24 years, from 1986 until 2010, there were no mortal encounters with grizzlies in Yellowstone National Park. But four deadly incidents over the past two summers have hikers on edge, reigniting the fierce debate over bear management.*

And Still More Aggressive Animals

After looking at a couple specific species on the attack in America with greater frequency there are articles I have found that indicate coyotes, wild cats, and assorted wild animals and even strange bugs are an instrument of judgment on the unfaithful land.

Coyote Attacks on the rise in Los Angeles: Meeting September 5[16]— examiner.com

ON THE LOOSE: URBAN COYOTES THRIVE IN NORTH AMERICAN CITIES[17]—Research News COLUMBUS, Ohio

> *Even in the largest American cities, a historically maligned beast is thriving, despite scientists' belief that these mammals intently avoid urban human populations. This animal's amazing ability to thrive in metropolitan areas has greatly surprised scientists, says Stanley Gehrt, an assistant professor of environmental and natural resources at Ohio State University. Gehrt is in the sixth year of a multi-year study of coyote behavior in urban Chicago.*

"We couldn't find an area in Chicago where there weren't coyotes," Gehrt said. "They've learned to exploit all parts of their landscape."

Animal Attacks Against Man on the Rise—ABCNews.com[18]

Cougar Attacks Increasing in West[19]

> *ISSAQUAH, Wash. (AP)—When concerns about marauding cougars rise, wildlife experts offer reassurances: The typical cougar is a shy creature that avoids people and prefers to eat deer rather than pets or children.*

So much for typical. Now consider the cougar that ate Wes Collins' dog:

> *It emerged from the forest behind the Collins house one evening in May and zeroed in on Sandy, the family's 50-pound Labrador mix. As two of Collins' children watched from the doorway, the cougar chased Sandy around the house and cornered her by the back deck. Clamping its jaws around the dog's neck, the cougar dragged Sandy 50 yards into the woods. There it gnawed on her*

head and shoulder, buried the rest for later, and stretched out for a long nap. That was enough to shake up the Collinses, but what happened the next day was what troubled state game warden Rocky Spencer. He and a hunter arrived with two hounds, pessimistic about their chances of tracking the cat. Collins' house sits on 5 acres outside Issaquah, where Seattle's suburban sprawl gives way to the forested Cascade foothills, so the cougar had plenty of escape routes to wilder country. But this cat had no intention of fleeing. The hounds came across it just 100 yards into the woods, and the snarling cougar turned on the dogs with a fury that sent both back to the truck to lick their wounds. Forty minutes later, hunter Ed Mahany returned with a friend and two fresh hounds. They figured that this time, surely, the cougar would have headed for the hills. Instead, the hounds found it just a few hundred feet away. Mahany's partner shot it, and the cougar, a 145-pound male, crawled off to die in a hollow stump that the neighbor's kids play in. "I've had dealings with upwards of 100 mountain lions, and that was the most aggressive I've seen," Spencer said. "This cougar wasn't sick or injured," Mahany added. "It obviously didn't concern him to be around people, and dogs were just lunch." Once hunted nearly to extinction, cougars are on the rebound around the West. It's an ecological success story that's causing both celebration and nervous glances over the shoulder. Worries are growing that the secretive cougar, a.k.a. mountain lion, puma and panther, is getting too comfortable around the booming human population that now shares its habitat. Of the 10 fatal cougar attacks on people recorded since 1890 in the United States, half were in the past 10 years. Nonfatal attacks also are on the rise, as are reports of cougars preying on pets and livestock.

Wild boars invade New York state; kill pets, chase people[20] — Reuters

Wild boar are invading the farms of central New York state, attacking livestock, killing family pets, chasing people and posing "devastating consequences" for the area, federal officials warn.

Frustrated Residents: Raccoons Slowly Taking Over New York City[21] CBS New York *"Some Who Live In Brooklyn Are Literally Having Their Lives Altered By Critters"*

SLEEP TIGHT—DON'T LET THE BEDBUGS BITE!

Unless you have been very busy with a project in your basement for the last five years and rarely come up for food or air you know about the bedbug infestations across America. Interestingly, one of the political parties, who also endorse same sex marriage and wholesale slaughter of babies, has bugs in the news tied to their national 2012 convention. Bedbugs suck blood from their host and these terrible sins are sucking the life out of America.

Bedbugs an increasing concern at DNC hotels[22]—The Washington Times
  Charlotte seeing an uptick in pest reports
  CHARLOTTE, N.C.—You think incumbent politicians are hard to get rid of? Try bedbugs. The blood-sucking insects have made a resurgence in recent years, including reports of them at nine

of the hotels being used for Democrats' nominating convention this week in Charlotte.

Whether it be bedbugs, tics, fleas, ants, stinkbugs, flies, wasps, killer Africanized bees, and that is just enough to help us get the idea, the bug problem in America is exploding! Pest control companies, veterinarians, homeowners, and most everyone else in our society is getting bugged like never before in America. Sadly, as we will see in the tenth chapter, many of these pests bring pestilence that is more than just annoying. According to Ezekiel the animals the Lord is using in judgment will de-populate regions of America. Now is a time to cry out to the Lord and run into *America's Ark!*

Mutated pests are quickly adapting to biotech crops in unpredicted and disturbing ways. It looks like that man might be creating some of the end-time plagues the Bible reports is coming. What fools these scientists are![23]

"Genetically modified crops are often designed to repel hungry insects. By having toxins built into the plant itself, farmers can reduce their use of environmentally unfriendly insecticide sprays. But as any first-year evolutionary biology student can tell you, insects are like the Borg in Star Trek: they quickly adapt. And this is precisely what is happening—but in ways that have startled the researchers themselves."

Can Pesticides Cause ADHD?

A study published today in the Journal of Pediatrics says that one type of pesticide commonly used on fruits and vegetables may be contributing to Attention Deficit Hyperactivity Disorder, or ADHD. Researchers took urine from over 1,000 participants ages 8 to 15 and analyzed it for pesticides. 119 of the children had symptoms of ADHD. Those with the highest concentration of pesticides were more likely to have the disorder, according to the study.[24]—ABC News

Of course these articles simply scratch the surface of what is going into our food supply today. However, it reminds us that the pests are influencing our health—again, this is just one example. The intensity of the bug problem has provoked our society to poison the bugs and thus, to some degree, poison ourselves!

When the Lord judges He is very creative—look at His awesome creation in judgment mode. Remember, though we hear all the natural reasons for the shark, bear, and other animal threatening situations, it is our Savior and God Messiah Jesus who is in charge of the animal kingdom—the One who rules over the Kingdom of God! So, if we look at things from His perspective, our eyes are open to what He is doing as it pertains to the second judgment given through Ezekiel—wild beasts or threatening animals. Thankfully, after each of these judgments our merciful Abba Father has a way forward and provides refuge for His people.

Prayerfully as we look at it together the Lord will grant us the wisdom to seek after grace and mercy that we may urgently enter in for protection from the storm—*America's Ark*!

Chapter 10

The Sword!

"Or if I bring a sword on that land, and say, 'Sword, go through the land,' and I cut off man and beast from it . . .
(Ezekiel 14:17)

O f all the chapters this is the most difficult for me to write. I have to be stripped of my bias as an American and fully look at the scripture as an unbiased representative of the Lord Jesus Christ. As His disciple my responsibility in regards to this chapter, along with all the others, is to tell the truth in love about the prophetic word of God coming to life in this generation of America. I expect to receive some criticism and anger as I share the truth regarding the Lord's sword upon America. I have found that following Jesus is often not "affirmation central."

Again, we have too often bought into a kind of fairy tale about the Lord, the world, and the generation in which we live. The truth is that when challenged, as God has been challenged by America, He will not back down and when it is His time the Lord will go to war. Additionally, the world is a very "not nice" place—there are plenty of folks who would love open doors of opportunity to do wrong in our neighborhoods, cities, states, and nation. This triangle (three points in this paragraph) is completed with the generation that sees God's prophetic word coming to pass that does not include America as a player in international scenarios. The three points in this triangle:

1) Most professing Christians in America have a fairy tale or unauthentic Western style of Christianity whereby the LORD does not judge wicked nations.
2) Many Americans are naïve regarding how violent the world is including the increasing widespread hatred of the USA.
3) America is not mentioned in Bible prophecy.

What does it mean when the Bible teaches that the Lord will bring a sword upon a land and its people? In simple terms it means that, along with all other facets of His creation, the Lord will judge with great destruction using mankind to kill those under judgment. We will see in scripture the pattern of the sword. Sadly, though it includes armies and war, there is much more to the "sword" that has been all around us in American society for many years.

Due to American Theology that "God only blesses America," it has been difficult to see what He is truly doing all around us. As before, I am only going to skim the surface, but I am confident you will get the picture, though it is sad to see. Please don't look away; there is great grace and mercy available for those who walk in the light of truth.

To establish clearly how the Lord judges with the sword, this chapter will have more Bible verses than any other. Due to the difficult-to-face realities for Americans, it is essential to have plenty of examples in the Bible to confirm this is the way of our Abba Father, Lord Jesus Christ, and Holy Spirit. We continually need to be reminded that the Bible is the best interpreter of the Bible.

The Lord Judges the Philistines for coming against Israel, led by King Saul, by turning their enemy's forces in against one another:

"Then Saul and all the people who were with him assembled, and they went to the battle; and indeed every man's sword was against his neighbor, and there was very great confusion. So the LORD saved Israel that day, and the battle shifted to Beth Aven." (1 Samuel 14:20,23)

The Lord judges King David with the sword against his family for his adulterous affair with Bathsheba and the murder of her husband, sending him to die by the Ammonite's sword. The "sword" included David's daughter Tamar being raped by her half-brother Amnon; he then was killed in revenge by his half-brother Absalom, and Absalom, David's son, was killed by David's soldiers after Absalom tried to kill David while trying to dethrone his father.

> *"Why have you despised the commandment of the LORD, to do evil in His sight? You have killed Uriah the Hittite with the sword; you have taken his wife to be your wife, and have killed him with the sword of the people of Ammon. Now therefore, the sword shall never depart from your house, because you have despised Me, and have taken the wife of Uriah the Hittite to be your wife." (2 Samuel 12:9–10)*

The Lord judges Assyrian King Sennacherib's army with the sword, and then him personally, for threatening Jerusalem.

> *"And Isaiah said to them, 'Thus you shall say to your master,"* *Thus says the LORD: 'Do not be afraid of the words which you have heard, with which the servants of the king of Assyria have blasphemed Me. Surely I will send a spirit upon him, and he shall hear a rumor and return to his own land; and I will cause him to fall by the sword in his own land.'" (2 Kings 19:6–7)*

> *Then the angel of the LORD went out, and killed in the camp of the Assyrians one hundred and eighty-five thousand; and when people arose early in the morning, there were the corpses— all dead. So Sennacherib king of Assyria departed and went away, returned home, and remained at Nineveh. Now it came to pass, as he was worshiping in the house of Nisroch his god, that his sons Adrammelech and Sharezer struck him down with the sword; and they escaped into the land of Ararat. Then Esarhaddon his son reigned in his place. (Isaiah 37:36–38)*

A multitude of enemies of Israel in a confederacy are turned in against one another—the sword!

"It happened after this that the people of Moab with the people of Ammon, and others with them besides the Ammonites, came to battle against Jehoshaphat. Then some came and told Jehoshaphat, saying, "A great multitude is coming against you from beyond the sea, from Syria; and they are in Hazazon Tamar" (which is En Gedi). (2 Chronicles 20:1–2)

Now when they began to sing and to praise, the LORD set ambushes against the people of Ammon, Moab, and Mount Seir, who had come against Judah; and they were defeated. For the people of Ammon and Moab stood up against the inhabitants of Mount Seir to utterly kill and destroy them. And when they had made an end of the inhabitants of Seir, they helped to destroy one another. So when Judah came to a place overlooking the wilderness, they looked toward the multitude; and there were their dead bodies, fallen on the earth. No one had escaped. (2 Chronicles 20:22–24)

The Lord raises up enemies to trouble King Solomon for his and Israel's sin.

"So the LORD became angry with Solomon, because his heart had turned from the LORD God of Israel, who had appeared to him twice, and had commanded him concerning this thing, that he should not go after other gods; but he did not keep what the LORD had commanded." (1 Kings 11:9–10)

"Now the LORD raised up an adversary against Solomon, Hadad the Edomite; he was a descendant of the king in Edom." (1 Kings 11:14)

"And God raised up another adversary against him, Rezon the son of Eliadah, who had fled from his lord, Hadadezer king of Zobah." (1 Kings 11:23)

Folks, these judgments from the Lord with the sword—do they sound like the Jesus Christ you know? This is the One whose prophetic words are coming to pass on America!

Violence

The violence in American cities began to spike as America started to war with the Holy One of Israel. Remember, Jesus Christ is the Holy One of Israel. And as He was kicked out of schools, court rooms, religion, government, economic business, and now alarmingly the U.S. military, the sword is falling across America from every quarter! We have learned to ignore and accept that the USA is now more than most could have ever imagined a very dangerous place.

I meet people from all over the world when travelling to many countries leading mission trips to share the gospel of Jesus Christ. Often on flights I strike up conversations with many interesting folks from European, Asian, and African countries. On such a flight I was speaking to a surgeon from the Netherlands who said this: "I would not like to visit America, yours is a very violent country." You see, he is on the outside looking in and not accustomed to such danger and violence that we have learned to accept as normal.

Mega church pastor beaten to death with electric guitar by man who rammed car into church.[1] Mail Online—A North Texas congregation is reeling after an attacker rammed a car into a church wall, chased the pastor, and beat him to death with an electric guitar.

American Cities

When I was a child growing up in America in the 1960s and '70s I could leave in the morning by myself on my bicycle and come back whenever without anyone thinking twice about my safety. Those days are long gone! While my almost-grown children were coming up in the '90s and 2000s I would not let them out of my sight! With the pedophiles, gun packing drug dealers and gang members, mass murder shooters at schools, movie theatres and every other "open season" public venue, sex traffickers, and other crazies that have become part of the fabric of American society, it has been a source of constant prayer to raise kids safely in this shark-infested "new normal."

All American major cities like New York, Chicago, Los Angeles, Houston, Atlanta, Miami, Detroit, and even mid-size and small rural cities and towns, are full of violent crime like never before. Again, this is a direct result of America declaring war on the Lord with the "Big Three" discussed in previous chapters along with the extreme exalting of all kinds of wickedness. I believe much of the violence is the sword the Lord promises the sinfully, persistently, unfaithful land who has had the knowledge of the true and living God and rejected Him and His ways. It is a society that He has turned in on itself.

"The wicked prowl on every side, When vileness is exalted among the sons of men." (Psalm 12:8)

Enter At Your Own Risk: Police Union Says 'War-Like' Detroit Is Unsafe For Visitors[2]—Local CBS Detroit

Chicago police confirm 'tragic number' of 500 homicides

Chicago Surpasses Last Year's Total[3]—CBS Chicago

Queens father fatally crushed by train after deranged man flings him onto Midtown subway tracks[4]—NYPOST.com

Police: Execution Style Slayings Leave 4 Dead In Detroit[5]—CBS Detroit

NYPD: Suspect Attacked, Robbed 85-Year-Old Woman In Elevator[6]—CBS New York

Man brutally shot in head in broad daylight in Midtown[7]—NYPOST.com

Man and woman found bound and gagged on San Francisco street[8]—U.S. News

Clackamas Town Center shooting: At least 2 shot dead, more injured by man with rifle[9] —OregonLive.com

Mother killed right outside Brookdale Hospital, where she was visiting sick daughter[10]—NYPOST.com

Sources: Multiple Deaths, Including Children, At Sandy Hook School Shooting In Newtown[11]—Time Newsfeed

Terrorist Attacks

While I was growing up in those final years of relative safety, compared to now, I remember my grandparents and parents watching the news and seeing terrorist attacks on European and other nations' soil including airplane hijackings, bombings, and shootings. The European nations had already been working against Israel very aggressively and the United States was much less so until 1991. Then later in the '90s the American, Israeli, Palestinian Oslo Accords prompted Yasser Arafat to receive the Nobel Peace Prize—Ha! Our beloved USA helped promote the father of modern-day terrorism to win the world's most prestigious peacemaker recognition!

It was this slippery slope that prompted the Holy One of Israel to bring the sword of terrorism to America. In a moment there will be an inclusive list of nations judged with the sword. In light of the verses we have seen, it would be naïve to believe that the Lord judged them with the sword, but that it is different when the sword comes to America in its time of unprecedented horrible sins: Israel, Ammonites, Moabites, Edomites, Babylon, Persia, Greece, Rome, and all other empires that have ever been brought down by the sword according to previous verses mentioned.

Wars

Consider the modern wars and skirmishes that have taken place involving America. Vietnam was during the initiation of the great rebellion of kicking Jesus Christ out of American schools, the "free love" or, more accurately said, fornication movement (any sex outside of marriage is fornication) that later helped facilitate the radical homosexual movement, and the momentum and realization of legalizing abortion. Sex outside of marriage produces unwanted babies. So, the obvious answer for those who walk in such darkness is to kill the babies. Again, I used to walk in such darkness, and but for God's grace would still be in such darkness.

Iraq and Afghanistan

Our Western way of thinking including fighting a war is so different than the Middle Eastern and Muslim mentality. We think like this: You have an overwhelming force with a gun to their head, they agree to terms, you then make peace and build up their society with infrastructure, government, business, and they become nice trading partners for the USA. Just look at Japan, and Germany right?

The problem starts with the gun to their head. They still negotiate with a gun to their head and believe that if you pull the trigger they receive virgins and rewards in heaven from Allah. They are so good at this game that they talk the guy who has a gun to their head out of his wallet! The only way to win is with overwhelming force. This is how America used to win wars, which has become a politically correct "no-no", and they know it.

And the historical fact is that America decimated Germany and erased two entire Japanese cities from the map before they would agree to terms. America doesn't win wars like that anymore. But, for the radical Muslim leaders war is still hell until you destroy the enemy of Islam. Theirs' really is a "win or die trying" philosophy.

That being established, American victory is replaced by a slow death with an endless torturous trickle of casualties and a bottomless black hole which consumes money and every other resource necessary to win. This creates war fatigue, which drains an empire of any heart to fight in current or any future wars. The price for endless unwinnable war simply becomes too high, and the world power has no will and fewer resources to maintain the military capacity of "empire" status. Such is the way for so many super powers in history under the sword of the LORD.

Taliban mock US as Afghan war enters 12th year[12]—Freerepublic.com
   America's longest war entered its 12th year Sunday, with the anniversary marked by a Taliban statement claiming that NATO forces are "fleeing Afghanistan" in "humiliation and disgrace."

In the book of Daniel we find the account of the Babylonian Empire's fall to the Medes and Persians that took place in one night. Of course this was God's prophetic judging by the sword. The Lord speaks through the Prophet Isaiah of the Persian King Cyrus approximately one hundred fifty years before his birth. What a book— the Bible! Cyrus would wield the sword of the Lord to bring down Babylon:

"Thus says the LORD to His anointed, To Cyrus, whose right hand I have held— To subdue nations before him And loose the armor of kings, To open before him the double doors, So that the gates will not be shut: 'I will go before you And make the crooked places straight; I will break in pieces the gates of bronze And cut the bars of iron. I will give you the treasures of darkness And hidden riches of secret places, That you may know that I, the LORD, Who call you by your name, Am the God of Israel." *(Isaiah 45:1–3)*

The King of Babylon Belshazzar had brought the holy instruments from the Temple in Jerusalem that had been captured earlier when the Southern Kingdom of Judah was judged by the sword of the Lord. Belshazzar, who was having a pagan, drunken party and shaking his fist at the Lord, decided to use the holy vessels to drink from—mocking the Holy One of Israel.

Belshazzar the king made a great feast for a thousand of his lords, and drank wine in the presence of the thousand. While he tasted the wine, Belshazzar gave the command to bring the gold and silver vessels which his father Nebuchadnezzar had taken from the temple which had been in Jerusalem, that the king and his lords, his wives, and his concubines might drink from them. Then they brought the gold vessels that had been taken from the temple of the house of God which had been in Jerusalem; and the king and his lords, his wives, and his concubines drank from them. They drank wine, and praised the gods of gold and silver, bronze and iron, wood and stone. (Daniel 5:1–4)

Tragically, this reminds me of homosexual marriage, evolution, pagan religion, and many other mockings of God being flaunted in the Lord's face today in America. But there are none so evil as the one about to be mentioned. The Holy Bible is the written word of the Living Holy One of Israel. Look down into the pit of wickedness expressed by the new homosexual Bible:

"Queen James Bible": Now There's a Gay-Friendly Version of Scripture[13]*—defendproclaimthefaith.org*

"The Queen James Bible resolves any homophobic interpretations of the Bible, but the Bible is still filled with inequality and even contradiction that we have not addressed," the web site notes. "No Bible is perfect, including this one. We wanted to make a book filled with the word of God that nobody could use to incorrectly condemn God's LGBT children, and we succeeded."

Well, the Holy One of Israel had an answer for the wicked Babylonian King and be reminded that He also has one for the wickedness in America today:

"In the same hour the fingers of a man's hand appeared and wrote opposite the lampstand on the plaster of the wall of the king's palace; and the king saw the part of the hand that wrote. Then the king's countenance changed, and his thoughts troubled him, so that the joints of his hips were loosened and his knees knocked against each other." (Daniel 5:5–6)

Daniel Interprets the Writing

And you have lifted yourself up against the Lord of heaven. They have brought the vessels of His house before you, and you and your lords, your wives and your concubines, have drunk wine from them. And you have praised the gods of silver and gold, bronze and iron, wood and stone, which do not see or hear or know; and the God who holds your breath in His hand and owns all your ways, you have not glorified. Then the fingers of the hand were sent from Him, and this writing was written. "And this is the inscription that was written:

MENE, MENE, TEKEL, UPHARSIN.

This is the interpretation of each word. MENE: God has numbered your kingdom, and finished it; TEKEL: You have been weighed in the balances, and found wanting; PERES: Your kingdom has been divided, and given to the Medes and Persians." *Then Belshazzar gave the command, and they clothed Daniel with purple and put a chain of gold around his neck, and made a proclamation concerning him that he should be the third ruler in the kingdom. That very night Belshazzar, king of the Chaldeans, was slain. And Darius the Mede received the kingdom, being about sixty-two years old. [Daris was the Medo leader while Cyrus was the Persian as they jointly conquered and rule]. (Daniel 5:23–31)*

Here is what we need to understand and consider as it relates to America. Most often world powers are in decline for a while before their sudden fall. History reports that Babylon had many regional fires they were unable to extinguish in their empire before they fell that one evening. The vulnerability of this inability to control the world as they once could stirs up a tumultuous vacuum of power until another empire rises up to finally bring them down and take their place.

I strongly believe the final Gentile Empire, led by the Anti-Christ spoken of by the Prophet Daniel and Apostle John in Revelation, is on its way up while the waning American super power is on its way down. Of course, that kingdom will be short lived, as it will be replaced by the final Kingdom ruled by our soon coming King Messiah Jesus! What a grand and glorious day that will be!

The USA is very vulnerable now that the military has officially made the exchange of the Lord Jesus Christ for homosexuality. The military will be gutted financially, drawn down numerically, destroyed in its morale as it has lost its morality, and defeated militarily. I say this with great sorrow in my heart. These are hard words to think and say. There will be "black eyes" given to the U.S. militarily all over the world.

Unthinkably, this will probably end up with our own armed forces turning in against its citizens by the time this downward spiral is complete—possibly even persecuting believers in Jesus. Christians certainly are ripe for persecution and are being so persecuted inside the military now. The born-again chaplains are being chased out for preaching, teaching, and praying in Jesus's name, while simultaneously, though there are regulations against it, pressured to oversee same-sex marriage ceremonies.

In What Have We Trusted?

Printed on our American currency is a phrase that, if it were true, would have prevented us from so much of this trouble: "In God We Trust." Instead, we have learned to trust in our great military power that has been, especially in the last twenty five years, unmatched by any other armed force on the planet. Placing our trust in physical weapons is folly because they will not help us fight the spiritual war in which we find ourselves engaged! Banking on our American military might prevents many from remembering to first trust our Lord Jesus. Yet there is a very important Bible verse that we born again followers of Jesus Christ need to remember:

"Some trust in chariots, and some in horses; But we will remember the name of the LORD our God." (Psalm 20:7)

Yet in all this the hand of the Lord is outstretched still to give grace and mercy to Americans even during this time of judgment with the sword. The way of escape has been provided which thankfully is available to "whosoever will" seek this place of heavenly refuge. There is one more judgment to discuss and then on to *America's Ark!*

Chapter 11

Pestilence

"Or if I send a pestilence into that land and pour out My fury on it in blood, and cut off from it man and beast . . ." (Ezekiel 14:19)

*I*f you were to ask the average Egyptian what was going on as the plagues from the Lord began to fall on their land, the last thing they would have believed is that the God of the Jews was punishing them for declaring war on Him. Yet the Bible tells us that is exactly what He was doing. Of course, the judgment on America is not as intense as that upon Egypt—yet. But, it will be, not only for America, but the entire world, and that time is not very far away. The point is that the folks in Egypt, all the way up to the top, mocked the God of Israel and would not acknowledge Him in the judgments until great devastation had come to Egypt.

The LORD Speaks With Moses

"Then you shall say to Pharaoh, 'Thus says the LORD: "Israel is My son, My firstborn. So I say to you, let My son go that he may serve Me. But if you refuse to let him go, indeed I will kill your son, your firstborn." (Exodus 4:22–23)

You see, unlike almost nineteen centuries of empires rising and falling from 70 AD onward to 1948, Israel was not an obvious component of world events. I say obvious because Israel is always on the mind of the God of Israel (Psalm 121:4). But now almost the entire world including America is attempting, at the very least, to put Israel in an extremely dangerous situation. This is no game and threatens its existence—the Lord has taken up the challenge! For many years America experienced great blessings for blessing Israel, but things have been changing in that regard.

In the same way Egypt experienced great blessings under Joseph and also for blessing Jacob and his descendants. Then things changed and Egypt declared war on Israel's God by coming against the children of Israel. So, like Egypt and many others who have experienced plagues of judgment, the plagues are upon the USA. And, by way of reminder, cursing Israel is only one of the "Big Three." Yet before looking at pestilence in America, it is first important to define it from a Bible perspective.

Pestilence is a fast-spreading deadly disease or plague that often involves animals or livestock. Our Lord Jesus predicted it as one of the signs of the birth pains that point to His imminent return as the Reigning King of the Universe from His headquarters in Jerusalem.

"For nation will rise against nation, and kingdom against kingdom. And there will be famines, pestilences, and earthquakes in various places. All these are the beginning of sorrows (birth pains)." (Matthew 24:7–8)

Today in America the pestilences are off the charts! They are coming from many origins and in many shapes, sizes, degrees of severity, and the names of some of them are even very frightening and telling.

I live in Texas, which is, at the time of this writing, the capital of West Nile Virus in America. Dallas has reported more West Nile deaths than anywhere in the country. The Houston area, where I currently live, was the second highest in Texas after Dallas. The number of deaths are reported on the news frequently, and this debilitating mosquito-borne slow painful killer is on the rise across the country. Few have yet associated the name West Nile with the plagues of Egypt. How ironic that this pestilence, which is now in all the forty eight continental United States, has the name of the river the Lord cursed in one of the plagues in Egypt (Exodus 7: 14–18).

Once again, news headlines can bring home the reality of things going on in today's world all around us:

Dallas mayor declares emergency over West Nile virus[1]—Reuters

Dallas launches aerial defense to fight West Nile virus[2]—Fox News

West Nile outbreak largest ever in U.S.[3]—CNN.com

Manhattan to be sprayed against West Nile virus[4]—Medical Express

CDC: More than 1,100 cases of West Nile reported through August[5]—Fox News

West Nile virus cases rise 40 percent in one week[6]—myfoxny.com
All 48 states w nile

West Nile Virus Cases Set Record, Deaths Soar[7]—Huffington Post

Killer Anti-Biotic Resistant Super Bugs:

There are unstoppable strains of anti-biotic resistant bacteria that are striking with horrifying scenarios:

NIH superbug claims 7th victim[8]—The Washington Post
A deadly, drug-resistant superbug outbreak that began last summer at the National Institutes of Health Clinical Center claimed its seventh victim Sept. 7, when a seriously ill boy from Minnesota succumbed to a bloodstream infection, officials said Friday.

Hanta Virus Pulmonary Syndrome

This pestilence is contracted by contact with rodent feces, urine, and saliva or inhaling airborne particles. It is fatal in thirty percent of cases.

Second person dies after contracting rare rodent-borne disease at Yosemite[9]—Fox News

CDC says 10,000 at risk of hantavirus in Yosemite outbreak[10]—Reuters

Third Yosemite visitor dies of hantavirus; eight now infected[11]—latimes.com

Bubonic Plague and Tuberculosis

Often when I travel to Africa people ask me if I am afraid to catch a disease over there. I have two testimonies that demonstrate how asleep we are to the reality of the USA plague dangers. The question regarding my safety in Africa compared to America demonstrates how we have not yet awakened to our own dangers here. The first testimony is very personal to me.

It was in the early 2000s when in my late 30s I developed what the doctors told me was asthma. This was long before I had been involved in international gospel work. I began using prescribed inhalers three or more times daily so that I could breathe. It was very unpleasant and sometimes drove me to prayer to avoid anxiety, yet the last thing I imagined was that it could have been deadly. I began crying out to the Lord for healing and literally and miraculously my Savior and Great Physician Jesus Christ healed me! I never used a breather again!

Approximately six years later while being "prepped" for shoulder surgery the attending medical folks did an x-ray on my lungs. They found strange knots in my lungs and suggested I go look into it. I did so and to make a long story short these things on my lungs were the leftover scars from the misdiagnosed tuberculosis that my Lord Jesus saved me from those many years earlier! Think of it: I take shots before leaving, and thankfully I have visited many countries in Africa without catching tuberculosis. However, I did contract the deadly disease in America!

The other testimony involves a mission trip I led to Rwanda and the DRC (Democratic Republic of Congo). Twelve of us were on our way back from a glorious time of seeing people come to Messiah Jesus to be saved along with assorted ministries to many hurting souls. While on layover in an airport in Qatar I was ambitiously looking at the Web News, having been out of the world events loop for two weeks. I found an astonishing article with gruesome pictures that reminded me how necessary it was to write this book!

It was an Oregon man who caught bubonic or Black Plague from a mouse bite in 2012. His hands and feet were swollen and black, and his fingers and toes had to be amputated. This pestilence killed 70–100 million people in China and Europe the 1300s. What strange things are cropping up in the USA and as rodent populations explode, Lord only knows what diseases will crop up with them. Folks, this is here in America! It is a true thing—individuals, like nations, also reap what they sow and what they plant is what will grow.

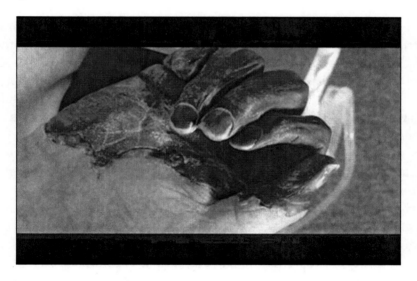

Colorado girl recovering from bubonic plague[12]—Fox News
  Plague is generally transmitted to humans through the bites of infected fleas but also can be transmitted by direct contact with infected animals, including rodents, rabbits and pets.

Frustrated UWS Resident Hangs "Rat Crossing" Signs—NBC News [13]

HIV And New AIDS-Like Dangers!

Let's reason about something together, HIV and AIDS primarily strikes those in America who have sex outside of marriage with the highest rates among the ones practicing homosexual behavior. Of course IV drug users are also at high risk. Does this not fit in with all we are seeing regarding the judgment of the Lord? Having made this point, here is a question: Is not the capital city of an empire to embody all its society represents?

In the 1970s my father, who was a trial lawyer, took me at ten years of age to Washington D.C. as he had a case at the Supreme Court. I will never forget the general meaning of the answer to my father's question regarding where we should go to dinner that night. The hotel concierge told us something to the effect that if you value you and your son's life don't leave the hotel after dark.

Much of the judgment falling on America is condensed in Washington D.C. Just look at this article regarding their HIV rates—-this is really scary!

AIDS epidemic in Washington[14]—DC Public Radio International
Washington, DC, has the dubious distinction of being America's AIDS capital, with the highest HIV infection rate in the country. A recent study estimated that the infection rate in DC is three

percent, the highest in the US. To put that figure in perspective, the Centers for Disease Control and the World Health Organization consider a one percent infection rate as the threshold for a severe epidemic.

While the national infection rate is well below that one percent threshold, in some cities, like Washington, DC, the problem is enormous. "If we know that three percent are currently diagnosed, the underlying number is probably five and six, or closer to five percent," said Dr. Ray Martins, Chief Medical Officer at the Whitman-Walker Clinic, the largest provider of HIV care in the nation's capital. "Our rates here in the District of Columbia are unbelievably, remarkably and unacceptably high for HIV," said Dr. Shannon Hader, Director of DC's HIV/AIDS Administration. DC's rates, she says, are comparable to those of countries in West Africa. She believes the city faces a number of challenges that are more pronounced in the US—and DC—in particular. "We have every risk factor there is, or every mode of transmission that there is," said Hader. "Whether it's heterosexual sex; whether it's men having sex with men; whether it's injection drug use—all of those three modes of transmission are all generating all new infections.

Along with almost incurable superbugs here are some more diseases that pose "AIDS-like" concerns:

African monkey meat that could be behind the next HIV—Health News—Health & Families[15]—The Independent

Chagas Disease, an incurable infection, called the 'new AIDS of the Americas'[16]—NY Daily News Disease is a parasitic infection transmitted by blood-sucking insects, largely in impoverished areas.

Deadly flesh-eating bacteria claims first life as sixth case of killer infection is identified. Woman pastor DIES after contracting flesh-eating bug in SIXTH case of deadly bacteria identified in America[17]— Mail Online

Other AIDS-Like Sexually Transmitted Diseases

Of course with the sexual revolution against our Creator Lord Jesus came the spike in STDs. The price for this rebellion is worsening quickly in that the deadly nature of those once easily treatable infections are becoming more deadly and treatment resistant:

Drug-Resistant Gonorrhea: Is The Antibiotic Era Coming To An End?[18]—Huffington Post
> *It really is as scary as it sounds. Gonorrhea is the newest superbug. Could it become the next AIDS? If you've never heard of a superbug before, you may want to sit down. It's a bit of an oversimplification, but bacteria and other infectious agents earn superbug status once they've developed resistance to a number of medications originally designed to wipe them out (like antibiotics). Methicillin-resistant Staphylococcus aureus (commonly called MRSA) falls into that category. And perhaps the newest member of the superbug family? Gonorrhea.*

This list with news articles is certainly not comprehensive, but here are more American pestilences that remind me of the need for a place of protection:

Dengue Fever

Dengue re-emerges in Florida[19]—USA Today
> *A water sample is teeming with mosquito larvae after it was collected from a fountain outside a vacant house July 15 in Miami Beach Miami-Dade County health officials are reporting the first suspected local case of dengue fever, a potentially serious mosquito-borne illness that had once disappeared from the United States.*

Dengue fever confirmed in Florida girl[20]—USA Today

Two recent guests of a Chicago Marriott have died after contracting Legionnaires' disease[21]—chicagotribune.com

Study Links Cat Litter Box to Increased Suicide Risk[22]—ABC News -
  Cat parasite linked with higher women suicide rates
  According to a new study, a parasite that lives in the gut of a cat
  may make infected women more prone to suicide.

Flea-Borne Typhus Reported On The Rise In Orange County[23]—CBS
Los Angeles

Woman Who Contracted Bacterial Infection Caused By Dog's Saliva
Dies[24]—CBS Atlanta

New Species Of Ticks Spreading Disease Across Southeast[25]—CBS
Charlotte
  CHAPEL HILL, N.C. (AP)—In the trees and grasses of the South,
  there are a growing number of unwanted visitors that at best
  are an itchy nuisance and at worst can carry debilitating dis-
  eases: Ticks. Public health officials say that numbers of reported
  cases of diseases like Lyme disease and Rocky Mountain spotted
  fever are not yet alarming and have not yet shown a definitive
  trend upward from a national perspective. But they do worry
  that more ticks means more of a risk that those diseases will
  spike.

Toxic green slime has taken over the lakes of America. Again[26]—
Grist.org
  Actually, this is not algae—it is bacteria. The organism is poi-
  sonous and has a terrible stench. Environmentalists' studies
  tell us it comes from a combination of farmers' fertilizers/
  pesticides and heavy rains in some of the areas affected. The
  news program *60 Minutes* aired a segment dedicated to the
  blue/green sludge explaining that recently it killed a family
  dog in a Wisconsin lake at which time an expert on the subject warned that human deaths were just around the corner.
  The blue/green plague covers lakes across America keeping
  people away from the regions affected by it. Just like Ezekiel
  warns man and beast are being cut off from American lakes
  due to this noxious plague!

"Or if I send a pestilence into that land and pour out My fury on it in blood, and cut off from it man and beast . . ." (Ezekiel 14:19)

These pestilences are ramping up, causing more sickness and death, and the Lord is using them to judge and bring people, whom He loves and died for, to a place of repentance. Even in judgment He remembers mercy and here is why. Even in wrath and judgment, expressing His holy and just nature, God is love. He loves people and wants them to turn from their sin. He always provides a place of shelter from the storms. And so it is in America's time of tempestuous stormy days. Please join me and let's learn how to "run for it" into *America's Ark.*

Chapter 12

America's Ark: Righteousness Like Noah, Daniel, and Job

"Even if these three men, Noah, Daniel, and Job, were in it, they would deliver only themselves by their righteousness," says the Lord GOD. (Ezekiel 14:14)

*H*ere we stand, at the place provided for us by our Great Savior Jesus—*America's Ark*. I call it so because the Ark represents the only place of safety from the comprehensive judgment of the Lord. There is only one place of protection provided for those in the unfaithful land under His outstretched hand. What is that provision of life? Let's read Ezekiel's prophecy again and begin to learn and understand the way, the truth, and the life!

> The word of the LORD came again to me, saying: "Son of man, when a land sins against Me by persistent unfaithfulness, I will stretch out My hand against it; I will cut off its supply of bread, send famine on it, and cut off man and beast from it. Even if these three men, Noah, Daniel, and Job, were in it, they would deliver only themselves by their righteousness," says the Lord GOD.
>
> "If I cause wild beasts to pass through the land, and they empty it, and make it so desolate that no man may pass through because of

the beasts, even though these three men were in it, as I live," says the Lord GOD, "they would deliver neither sons nor daughters; only they would be delivered, and the land would be desolate.

"Or if I bring a sword on that land, and say, 'Sword, go through the land,' and I cut off man and beast from it, even though these three men were in it, as I live," says the Lord GOD, "they would deliver neither sons nor daughters, but only they themselves would be delivered.

"Or if I send a pestilence into that land and pour out My fury on it in blood, and cut off from it man and beast, even though Noah, Daniel, and Job were in it, as I live," says the Lord GOD, "they would deliver neither son nor daughter; they would deliver only themselves by their righteousness." (Ezekiel 14:12–20)

At the end of each warning of severe judgment we see that the righteousness of Noah, Daniel, and Job is the *only* means of deliverance from the heavy hand of the Lord! This life preserver is not a life raft—it only has room for one. This Ark, unlike the one in Noah's day, only takes reservations for one. You cannot accurately say "my father or mother walk like Noah, Daniel, and Job, and since I live in their house or I am their child the Lord will keep me from the storm." No, only a person's individual righteousness like that of Noah, Daniel, and Job will help in these and the soon-coming days.

The most obvious question before going any further is the Biblical definition of "righteousness." So, here is a brief description. Speaking of the Hebrew root word for righteousness the Theological Wordbook of the Old Testament puts it nicely: "This root basically connotes conformity to an ethical or moral standard."[1] Of course the One who sets the standard for righteousness is the Lord. So, to conform to His standards set for His people of thinking, speaking, and living would be expressions of His righteousness. This would be impossible for any man except for two beautiful words: "BUT GOD"! The only way to attain to His standards is by the Holy One of Israel providing a lifesaving knowledge of Himself and graciously empowering His covenant people to live by His ways!

The LORD is righteous in all His ways, Gracious in all His works. (Psalm 145:17)

From here it is important for us to know the answer to some questions:

Of all the righteous people in the Bible, why Noah, Daniel, and Job? What is the righteousness of Noah, Daniel, and Job? They lived a long time ago—can their lives really be relevant to mine in America or anywhere in this world thousands of years later in the twenty-first century? How can I be righteous like these spiritual super heroes? These questions will certainly be answered as we continue.

Why Noah, Daniel, and Job?

Before looking at each of their lives individually let's notice some similarities between all three. These commonalities begin to answer the above question. First, all of them lived righteously through catastrophic times. They did so while most around them lived in such a way as to bring on great judgment and catastrophe. Noah, Daniel, and Job trusted in the Lord, which in the long run paid off with great reward. The short term was very difficult, and that trust came with great cost, yet we must remember that our Lord Jesus always saves the best for last!

For all three righteous men there was great temptation to stop and take the easier path—the one our Lord Jesus tells us leads to destruction! These common examples and experiences help us to see why it will take the righteousness of Noah, Daniel, and Job to make it through the days ahead. Let's prepare ourselves to enter *America's Ark* by learning about the righteousness of Noah.

What Did Noah Find That Americans Need Today?

The answer to this question begins to give us the understanding of the righteousness of Noah, Daniel, and Job, along with their relevance for our generation. We will also see that we too can be a Noah in some respects and like the others in Ezekiel's passage as well.

The world was in great sin with corruption and all forms of evil, and great violence was the order of the day. Polluted so much was the planet that almost all people were beyond repentance—too far gone to turn to the Lord. Oh, what a tragic time:

Then the LORD saw that the wickedness of man was great in the earth, and that every intent of the thoughts of his heart was only evil continually. And the LORD was sorry that He had made man on the earth, and He was grieved in His heart. So the LORD said, "I will destroy man whom I have created from the face of the earth, both man and beast, creeping thing and birds of the air, for I am sorry that I have made them." (Genesis 6:5–7)

The earth also was corrupt before God, and the earth was filled with violence. So God looked upon the earth, and indeed it was corrupt; for all flesh had corrupted their way on the earth. (Genesis 6:11–12)

In the midst of this oncoming catastrophic flood that would kill almost everyone on the planet there is a word that is wonderful for the righteous: BUT!

"But Noah found grace in the eyes of the LORD." (Genesis 6:8)

"But Noah found" is a great concept to understand as the flood of judgment is coming upon America! *"But Noah found"* means as the deluge of wrath was coming to the earth in Noah's day there was an exception to being in the category of those wiped out by it. Isn't that what you want to be in our time of judgment—an exception to those the Lord is judging? Don't you want to be able to say *"But I found,"* which spares you from the heavy hand of the Lord?

Some may say, "What America is facing today or even in the future won't be as bad as Noah's day." Oh really, with threat of things like famine on the land, or being killed by an animal or terrorist attack, or violence in our cities, or dying from one of these weird diseases, I think it will be plenty bad—it is, and will be a great joy to be able to say *"But I found!"*

The answer to the earlier asked question regarding what Noah found in the sixth chapter of Genesis is the most important life-giving gift to a world of sinners today. It is also found in the second chapter of the New Testament book of Ephesians:

"For by grace you have been saved through faith, and that not of yourselves; it is the gift of God, not of works, lest anyone should boast." (Ephesians 2:8–9)

The same thing that Noah found during a time of great wickedness and calamity we have available for us today—grace! Through the prophetic plans of God we look back to the cross and receive the grace provided by our Father who gave His only begotten Son Jesus Christ to die on the cross, rise again, and save us from our sins! We look back to the cross while Noah looked forward to Calvary where his sins would be ultimately paid for like ours. Until then Noah walked by the grace available in his day.

Remember what we are looking for here—it is the righteousness of Noah, Daniel, and Job. This is what will save us in our day like it did in theirs. We have just seen in the letter to the Ephesian church that grace saves, yet grace that saves comes to us through a conduit or avenue. Like a car needs a road to travel on, grace needs faith on which to travel. Faith gives us the roadway on which to ride in God's grace.

"But now the righteousness of God apart from the law is revealed, being witnessed by the Law and the Prophets, even the righteousness of God, through faith in Jesus Christ, to all and on all who believe." (Romans 3:21–22)

In this wonderful New Testament passage Paul wrote to the Roman believers that righteousness comes *through* faith in Jesus Christ! Do you see in this passage—grace through faith?

As many of us have heard, grace is the Lord's goodness given to undeserving sinners who simply receive it by faith to be saved from God's wrath. But grace is so much more—it is the goodness of the Lord that gives us the opportunity to know Him and be changed into His likeness—wow! As we receive our Lord Jesus and walk by His grace, the love of our Father, by the power of the Holy Spirit, changes us like a crawling caterpillar is changed into a beautiful airborne monarch butterfly! We become less like us and our dark environment, and we can reflect His goodness by the goodness He gives to us!

However, the grace Noah found and lived by is much different than what many call grace in America or the modern American brand of Christianity. This is something to address in detail later, but first let's look at the grace Noah found in his day, which is revealed even more in the New Covenant. And then may we learn how it can be the place of protection for me—us—today! Let's look at the grace Noah found and the fruit it produces proving it is true grace.

*"Either make the tree good and its **fruit** good, or else make the tree bad and its **fruit** bad; for a tree is known by its **fruit**." (Matthew 12:33, emphasis added)*

The first thing we can see regarding the fruit of the grace Noah found is that he heard from the Lord. There are two necessary components of this. The first is that the Lord is speaking to Noah. The God of the Bible constantly speaks to His children. People say today, "We are all God's children," implying that every human is a child of God. Well, as nice as that sounds, there is a politically incorrect verse that tells us that only the righteous are His children.

"In this the children of God and the children of the devil are manifest: Whoever does not practice righteousness is not of God, nor is he who does not love his brother." (1 John 3:10)

The second component regarding hearing from the Lord is that righteous Noah had a relationship with God such that not only did the Lord speak with Noah, but Noah heard from Him. This came in real handy to Noah and his family when it was time for mankind to be judged by the great flood.

"And God said to Noah, "The end of all flesh has come before Me, for the earth is filled with violence through them; and behold, I will destroy them with the earth. Make yourself an ark of gopherwood; make rooms in the ark, and cover it inside and outside with pitch." (Genesis 6:13–14)

Because Noah could hear from the Lord he learned about this life saving boat that it was time to get busy building. Notice, the others who perished did not hear from the Lord. Do you hear from the Lord Jesus today? Listen to our Savior speak to us from His holy word:

"My sheep hear My voice, and I know them, and they follow Me." (John 10:27)

Those who have been made righteous by repenting of their sin, and believing in our Lord Jesus Christ alone to be saved, hear His voice. They hear Him in prayer by the Holy Spirit who dwells within, or as the Holy Spirit brings revelation from the Word of God the Bible, or by those in authority like husbands, pastors, bosses, and others, and through godly relationships like wives, children, brothers and sisters in Christ, and also by Abba Father's loving hand operating through circumstances in their lives.

The next thing that I will point out is seen above in 1 John 3:10. It is this simple—we know Noah was righteous because the Lord spoke to him, he heard from the Lord, then he practiced righteousness by obeying the Lord. I am confident that like any other created man he did not obey Him perfectly, but the order of his life was to build that boat. You see, those made righteous by grace through faith follow the Shepherd and practice righteousness!

And behold, I Myself am bringing floodwaters on the earth, to destroy from under heaven all flesh in which is the breath of life; everything that is on the earth shall die. But I will establish My covenant with you; and you shall go into the ark—you, your sons, your wife, and your sons' wives with you. And of every living thing of all flesh you shall bring two of every sort into the ark, to keep them alive with you; they shall be male and female. Of the birds after their kind, of animals after their kind, and of every creeping thing of the earth after its kind, two of every kind will come to you to keep them alive. And you shall take for yourself of all food that is eaten, and you shall gather it to yourself; and it shall be food for you and for them." Thus Noah did; according to all that God commanded him, so he did. (Genesis 6:17–22)

From these passages we can identify one of the very serious problems found in modern Americanized Christianity. Many believe that professing righteousness is enough, while the Bible is very clear in both the Old and New Testaments this is not the case. Remember, it is the righteousness of Noah that we are looking for here so that we can seek refuge in that same righteous faith during the current and coming storms to America.

"But someone will say, "You have faith, and I have works." Show me your faith without your works, and I will show you my faith by my works. You believe that there is one God. You do well. Even the demons believe—and tremble! But do you want to know, O foolish man, that faith without works is dead?" (James 2:18–20)

"Speaking of our Lord Jesus: . . . though He was a Son, yet He learned obedience by the things which He suffered. And having been perfected, He became the author of eternal salvation to all who obey Him . . ." (Hebrews 5:8–9)

We see in these two New Testament or New Covenant scriptures that the kind of grace which makes people righteous actually does something. It manifests or operates through the faith of the righteous individual and produces obedience to our Lord Jesus Christ. Grace that saves from the storm brings good Kingdom works that bear fruit for the Kingdom of God! That is the righteousness of Noah.

So, we have seen that the Lord spoke to Noah, he heard from the Lord, and he obeyed Him. Before moving on to the final and most exciting part of Noah's journey, let's take inventory together. Does the Lord Jesus Christ speak to you; do you hear His voice?

Do you obey Him? Do you read the Bible and do what it says with regard to living a holy life (1 Peter 1:15–17), sharing the gospel with the lost and making disciples of Jesus Christ (Matthew 28:18–20), wives obeying your husbands and husbands loving your wives (Ephesians 5:24,25), using your spiritual gifts in the body of Christ (1 Peter 4:10), and so on?

Think of this interesting point. We have heard the Lord's warning through Ezekiel's prophecy that sons or daughters cannot be saved by their mother or father's righteousness, but only by personal righteousness like Noah, Daniel, and Job. So, how was Noah's family saved?

Noah lived a righteous life before his wife, sons, and daughters in law. He told them what the Lord said and lived a personal life of consistent obedience to His words in front of them for one hundred and twenty years, the Bible tells us! He involved them in the Kingdom work giving them opportunity to practice righteousness as well. The Lord gave Noah's family grace and they believed in Him which provoked them to join Noah in the righteous work.

This is our first mission field—our own precious spouses, sons, and daughters. Let's live like Noah before them leading our families to righteous saving grace through faith in our Lord Jesus Christ! Noah's family being saved also shows us that you don't have to be a larger than life super hero to have the same kind of righteousness that saved Noah.

Next we will look at the most important and exciting part of Noah's righteous journey.

Noah's Inheritance

We know that when Noah and his family got off that boat they had inherited the entire earth! There was nobody else left. They were the progenitors of the planet and humanly speaking it all belonged to them. Yet look at what the Bible tells us: what Noah inherited was far better than the things of this world:

"By faith Noah, being divinely warned of things not yet seen, moved with godly fear, prepared an ark for the saving of his

household, by which he condemned the world and became heir of the righteousness which is according to faith." (Hebrews 11:7)

Do you see it? Noah had godly fear, something you don't see much in today's Christianity, he heard from the Lord, obeyed Him faithfully in building the ark, his family received the same lifesaving grace, by His righteous obedience he warned the world who would not listen, and from all this Noah became the heir of a great inheritance. What did he inherit? Noah received the great prize of all prizes—*righteousness*! This is exactly what we need according to the Lord through Ezekiel. The greatest reward in the universe is the righteousness of our Lord Jesus and we have seen together the blueprint to receive it along with Noah!

While American Christians have been duped into believing that the greatest prizes are prosperity, including such things as more money, cars, houses, and comfortable living in this world, there is a prize that living for those things can cause us to forfeit. The prize is righteousness in Jesus Christ that comes from taking up our cross, denying ourselves, and following our Lord Jesus!

> *Then Jesus said to His disciples, "If anyone desires to come after Me, let him deny himself, and take up his cross, and follow Me. For whoever desires to save his life will lose it, but whoever loses his life for My sake will find it. For what profit is it to a man if he gains the whole world, and loses his own soul? Or what will a man give in exchange for his soul? For the Son of Man will come in the glory of His Father with His angels, and then He will reward each according to his works. "Assuredly, I say to you, there are some standing here who shall not taste death till they see the Son of Man coming in His kingdom." (Matthew 16:24–28)*

Please take this time to ask our Father in heaven to give you an accurate appraisal of where you are with the Lord Jesus. Pray, confess your sins, be cleansed by the Lord Jesus (make sure He is your Lord and Savior), and be filled with His Holy Spirit. Ask Him to speak to you; listen for His voice in prayer, read His word, hear from authentic godly pastors and preachers, fellowship with other strong disciples of Jesus Christ, and obey Him in this dangerous, yet full of potential time in which the Lord has placed us.

Remember, *America's Ark* is the only place of refuge in this day and those soon coming. Let's continue to thankfully learn of *America's Ark* and how to run into it while there is yet a little time.

NOAH'S REFUGE PRINCIPLES

1) Noah Found Grace—the goodness of the Lord that gives God's righteousness to sinners!
2) Grace only comes through authentic faith in Jesus Christ!
3) The Lord spoke to Noah and Noah heard from the Lord!
4) Authentic righteous faith produces obedience to our Lord Jesus!
5) Fear of God that produces obedience warns the lost that judgment is coming!
6) Grace through faith produces fruit!
7) Grace through faith produces a righteous eternal inheritance!

Chapter 13

America's Ark – Righteousness Like Daniel

. . ."O Daniel, man greatly beloved . . . (Daniel 10:10)

*I*nterestingly, the name Daniel means Elohim or God is my Judge. The reason for interest is that as the Southern Kingdom of Israel was being judged by the Lord, and the people of Judah were dying or hopelessly being taken captive into Babylon, Daniel's personal character and testimony in heaven and earth was developing into a life that was beloved of the Lord! Isn't that what we want—as our nation and the world are under the judgment of the Lord Jesus Christ don't we want to be known as His beloved?

> *"In the third year of the reign of Jehoiakim king of Judah, Nebu-chadnezzar king of Babylon came to Jerusalem and besieged it. And the Lord gave Jehoiakim king of Judah into his hand, with some of the articles of the house of God, which he carried into the land of Shinar to the house of his god; and he brought the articles into the treasure house of his god." (Daniel 1:1–2)*

The Lord's prophets began warning Judah in the 700s BC with Isaiah, and then up to the time of judgment with Jeremiah, Ezekiel, and others. From 605 to 586 BC Babylon besieged Jerusalem three times, each with greater intensity and ferocity. The Bible tells us the conditions in Jerusalem were worse than we can imagine. Starvation, hopeless desperation, and even cannibalism, defined the Southern Kingdom of Judah.

The same One judging Judah with great expressions of wrath and fury not only had great mercy on Daniel, but raised him up into great positions of influence and notability in Babylon and Persia. Daniel wasn't a slick politician—to the contrary his political campaign was door knocking at the throne room of the Lord!

Do Not Love This World!

"Do not love the world or the things in the world. If anyone loves the world, the love of the Father is not in him. For all that is in the world—the lust of the flesh, the lust of the eyes, and the pride of life—is not of the Father but is of the world. And the world is passing away, and the lust of it; but he who does the will of God abides forever." (1 John 2:15–17)

The reason Daniel was so beloved of the Lord is that He loved the Heavenly City more than Babylon. From the beginning of his stay in Babylon he did something that demonstrated his love for the Lord more than his life in this world—he loved the Lord his God with all his heart, mind, soul, and strength! His inward love for the Lord burst outward as a visibly godly life! This included choosing Israel's God over Babylon.

Daniel's First Big Test

Then the king instructed Ashpenaz, the master of his eunuchs, to bring some of the children of Israel and some of the king's descendants and some of the nobles, young men in whom there was no blemish, but good-looking, gifted in all wisdom, possessing knowledge and quick to understand, who had ability to serve in the king's palace, and whom they might teach the language and literature of the Chaldeans. And the king appointed for them a daily provision of the king's delicacies and of the wine which he drank, and three years of training for them, so that at the end of that time they might serve before the king. Now from among those of the sons of Judah were Daniel, Hananiah, Mishael, and Azariah. To them the chief of the eunuchs gave names: he gave Daniel the name Belteshazzar; to Hananiah, Shadrach; to Mishael, Meshach; and to Azariah, Abed-Nego. (Daniel 1:3–7)

Daniel and his three Hebrew friends were very talented and gifted young men of the Lord. King Nebuchadnezzar was no dummy and wanted these special lads to lead in his kingdom. First though, he would have to erase their former identity and groom them to be Babylonian. The reason for the new Babylonian names was that all their Israeli names gave them identity as followers of the Holy One of Israel while the Babylonian ones identified them with the gods of Babylon. That is exactly what the Babylonian world system does to us today! This world system energized by Satan aggressively attempts to steal our identity as disciples of Jesus Christ. What should our response be?

"I beseech you therefore, brethren, by the mercies of God, that you present your bodies a living sacrifice, holy, acceptable to God, which is your reasonable service. ² And do not be conformed to this world, but be transformed by the renewing of your mind, that you may prove what is that good and acceptable and perfect will of God." (Romans 12:1–2)

As this identity theft process begins for Daniel he is faced with disobeying the Levitical statutes the Lord laid out for Israel in the Torah (Law). Yet, celebrate with heaven at his powerful love for the Lord! And also, begin to enter into the place of refuge with Daniel to share his steadfast faith.

"But Daniel purposed in his heart that he would not defile himself with the portion of the king's delicacies, nor with the wine which he drank; therefore he requested of the chief of the eunuchs that he might not defile himself." (Daniel 1:8)

What a huge insult this would be to the King—to reject the food from the Babylonian royal table! Didn't Daniel know what King Nebuchadnezzar had ruthlessly done to the peoples of so many other conquered nations? Didn't he see much of the same story unfolding for the rebels of Judah?

The Bible goes on to say that Daniel wisely and humbly asked the servant who was appointed to their care that he and his Hebrew brothers in the Lord might be given kosher (clean) food according to the Mosaic Law given to Israel. The choice was clear to Daniel: obey the Lord even to death if necessary or live the life of compromise and uncleanness (defilement) in Babylon.

> *Now God had brought Daniel into the favor and goodwill of the chief of the eunuchs. And the chief of the eunuchs said to Daniel, "I fear my lord the king, who has appointed your food and drink. For why should he see your faces looking worse than the young men who are your age? Then you would endanger my head before the king." So Daniel said to the steward whom the chief of the eunuchs had set over Daniel, Hananiah, Mishael, and Azariah, "Please test your servants for ten days, and let them give us vegetables to eat and water to drink. Then let our appearance be examined before you, and the appearance of the young men who eat the portion of the king's delicacies; and as you see fit, so deal with your servants." So he consented with them in this matter, and tested them ten days. And at the end of ten days their features appeared better and fatter in flesh than all the young men who ate the portion of the king's delicacies. Thus the steward took away their portion of delicacies and the wine that they were to drink, and gave them vegetables. (Daniel 1:9–16)*

This is so wonderful—look at what these righteous young men have done. They have basically said, "Well Lord it is up to you now. Our lives are in your hands as we have done all we can—the rest is up to You."

King David's words help remind us Who holds our lives and days:

"My times are in thy hand: deliver me from the hand of mine enemies, and from them that persecute me." (Psalm 31:15, KJV)

So the big day (ten) came, and we find the Lord's answer to Daniel's creative plea that he might live obediently to Him in Babylon. This would set the stage for one of the most exciting and impacting lives in human history! If Daniel compromises or dies so dies some of the greatest prophecies and revelations ever given to a man—with nothing comparable until those of John over five hundred years later in the book of Revelation. Think of it this way—Daniel's writings are coming to life in front of our eyes in this twenty-first century. When there is no America, there will be Daniel's words from the Lord!

Hallelujah! Daniel obeyed our Lord and was delivered by His faithful hand. He and the other three Hebrew boys continually were placed in tempting and life threatening situations yet unswervingly decided it would be better to die a death honoring the Lord than to live the life of compromise in Babylon.

What about us today? You see, Babylon represented everything the world has to offer. Every false and weird god and its religion, luxury and comfort, were embodied in one word—*Babylon*! And America is a kind of Babylon. The USA is not "the" Babylon of these end times as some assert, but today's America is a very close representation, type, and microcosm of it.

This is one of the reasons Daniel was so beloved of the Lord. As all the temptations of Babylon presented themselves to Daniel he consistently loved the Lord and chose Him over the pleasures of this life. Daniel realized he could not love both, but that he had to choose. So it is with us today in the Babylonian style of America of the twenty-first century. We have the same choices with our daily thinking, speaking, and living. Who and what will we love? Will it be the Lord Jesus Christ who gave Himself for us and the things of His Kingdom, or will we love this world and the things in it that are set against our precious Savior?

Remember, we are looking for the righteousness of Daniel as a place of refuge for us today. This is very important so please don't miss it: *What facilitated Daniel's righteous choice was that he had already learned to love the LORD with all his heart before his time of trouble in Babylon.* Daniel realized something—though he was in the world—*he was not of it!*

As mentioned above, the Lord used Babylon as His instrument of judgment on the Jewish people as their powerful forces besieged and burned Jerusalem along with taking many Jews captive. This would have been the most miserable time ever for the citizens of Judah. So it was for Daniel, yet by his righteous godly character Daniel overcame horrible pain and trouble, becoming one of the most extraordinary people to have ever lived! When I say pain and trouble think of this list: taken as a young teen from his family in Judah, brought to a land of strange language and customs, made a eunuch, according to some scholars, tempted often, endured life-threatening circumstances for his faith, and more!

How did Daniel go through all of this while refusing temptation and compromising steps to stay alive, or without giving up on the Lord? Again, though in Babylon he was not of it. Daniel recognized that he was a citizen of the Kingdom of the Lord. He had been placed there to bring glory to the God of Israel and to be a blessing to Babylon, Persia, and ultimately through the book of Daniel, many in the entire world for thousands of years!

Kingdom Citizenship

If there is anything American Christians are on the outside looking in at today, it is heavenly citizenship. So, in a nutshell here it is along with Scripture to confirm this brief explanation:

We are citizens of the Righteous Kingdom of Jesus Christ sent by the Righteous King to live in enemy territory to accurately represent His Glorious Kingdom. We are ambassadors sent from the King with a message of reconciliation—the gospel of Jesus Christ. All our resources, spiritual and physical, come from the King as we seek first His Kingdom and it's what? That is right—*righteousness*! We are to live in such a way that others learn about the King and leave the dominion of darkness to pledge and live allegiance to the

Kingdom of God. We are royal priests bringing more beloved citizens out of the darkness into His marvelous light!

"For our citizenship is in heaven, from which we also eagerly wait for the Savior, the Lord Jesus Christ . . ." (Philippians 3:20)

"Behold, I send you out as sheep in the midst of wolves. Therefore be wise as serpents and harmless as doves." (Matthew 10:16)

"Now then, we are ambassadors for Christ, as though God were pleading through us: we implore you on Christ's behalf, be reconciled to God. For He made Him who knew no sin to be sin for us, that we might become the righteousness of God in Him." (2 Corinthians 5:20–21)

"But seek first the kingdom of God and His righteousness, and all these things shall be added to you." (Matthew 6:33)

"Let your light so shine before men, that they may see your good works and glorify your Father in heaven." (Matthew 5:16)

"But you are a chosen generation, a royal priesthood, a holy nation, His own special people, that you may proclaim the praises of Him who called you out of darkness into His marvelous light . . ." (1 Peter 2:9)

DANIEL'S REFUGE PRINCIPLES

1) Love the Lord Jesus Christ with your whole life!
2) Do not love this world!
3) Purpose in your heart to not defile yourself!
4) Walk in humble obedience to our Lord Jesus!
5) Entrust your days to our heavenly Abba Father!
6) Trust Him today before worse trouble comes!
7) Learn Kingdom citizenship!
8) Hunger, thirst, and seek after righteousness!

Chapter 14

Daniel's Testimony

I was watching . . . (Daniel 7:13)

Watch Therefore!

S o many American Christians are looking for posh, pleasure, promotion, position, prestige, and a pile of money, but what was Daniel looking for? While the Babylonian culture had conformed its people into much the same mold as modern American Christianity today, what did the Lord show Daniel that he should be looking for with all his heart? Daniel believed in the coming of the Son of Man and looked for His glorious everlasting Kingdom!

> *"I was watching in the night visions, And behold, One like the Son of Man, Coming with the clouds of heaven! He came to the Ancient of Days, And they brought Him near before Him. Then to Him was given dominion and glory and a kingdom, That all peoples, nations, and languages should serve Him. His dominion is an everlasting dominion, Which shall not pass away, And His kingdom the one Which shall not be destroyed." (Daniel 7:13–14)*

Daniel knew that one day the great Son of Man, our Lord Jesus Christ, would come for His people in all His glory! King Jesus would then be presented to the Ancient of Days, our Holy Heavenly Father, and receive from the Father His everlasting Kingdom! I cannot help but use exclamation points for these statements—what GLORY—what a day that will be! Daniel thought so as well.

So much so, that Daniel was sold out for the King and His ever-lasting Kingdom. He lived a life of preparation and readiness to see the King coming for him in glory. Daniel spent his days watching and preparing for the King of kings and Lord of lords. Our Lord Jesus told us to do no less.

> *"Watch therefore, for you do not know what hour your Lord is coming." (Matthew 24:42)*

While our Lord Jesus was speaking about the signs that are all around us in this (our) generation He repeated what Daniel saw in his vision:

> *"Then they will see the Son of Man coming in a cloud with power and great glory. Now when these things begin to happen, look up and lift up your heads, because your redemption draws near." (Luke 21:27–28)*

Daniel was watching in the night visions and saw the coming of our Lord Jesus Christ. And a great place of refuge in these troubled times is to walk out the same righteous faith as Daniel by looking for the coming of the Lord! Even before these visions Daniel knew from the Torah to be watching for the Messiah of Israel (Deuteronomy 18:18).

Daniel's Testimony—Watching and Doing!

Our Lord Jesus was very clear that those who watch for His coming live as His righteous servants. It is kind of like this: "Watching for His coming provokes us to do what He commanded." Those who are watching are doing. These watching and Kingdom busy servants have something very powerful for a lost world to see—a *testimony*!

"Watch therefore, for you do not know what hour your Lord is coming. But know this, that if the master of the house had known what hour the thief would come, he would have watched and not allowed his house to be broken into. Therefore you also be ready, for the Son of Man is coming at an hour you do not expect." (Matthew 24:42–44)

The Watching Faithful Servant and the Negligent Evil Servant

Who then is a faithful and wise servant, whom his master made ruler over his household, to give them food in due season? Blessed is that servant whom his master, when he comes, will find so doing. Assuredly, I say to you that he will make him ruler over all his goods. But if that evil servant says in his heart, 'My master is delaying his coming,' and begins to beat his fellow servants, and to eat and drink with the drunkards, the master of that servant will come on a day when he is not looking for him and at an hour that he is not aware of, and will cut him in two and appoint him his portion with the hypocrites. There shall be weeping and gnashing of teeth. (Matthew 24:45–51)

The reason this so closely relates to Daniel is that no matter the situation or conditions his righteous watching for the coming Son of Man translated into Daniel serving Him with his life. And others took notice! Whether it was ministering to King Nebuchadnezzar by grace and miraculously interpreting his dreams, or Daniel accepting being sentenced to death in the lion's den instead of compromising by obeying the command of King Darius to not pray to the God of Israel, others were brought to knowledge of the Lord by Daniel's righteous testimony.

"Nebuchadnezzar the king, To all peoples, nations, and languages that dwell in all the earth: Peace be multiplied to you. I thought it good to declare the signs and wonders that the Most High God has worked for me. How great are His signs, And how mighty

His wonders! His kingdom is an everlasting kingdom, And His dominion is from generation to generation." (Daniel 4:1–3)

"Now I, Nebuchadnezzar, praise and extol and honor the King of heaven, all of whose works are truth, and His ways justice. And those who walk in pride He is able to put down." (Daniel 4:37)

Here we see the salvation of this pagan king as he is brought into the saving knowledge of the Holy One of Israel. How so? It was by the Lord's glorious power working through the authentic testimony of Daniel. That is an ark or place of refuge for you and me today! Many from Judah were killed or enslaved by the Babylonian ruler while righteous Daniel, without compromise of his faith, led the Babylonian King to Messiah Jesus!

The Medo-Persian Empire had conquered Babylon. King Darius realized how bad his prideful decision was to sign the law restricting anyone from praying unless their homage was to the king himself! This was a set-up by Daniel's adversaries in that they couldn't entrap him with any other wrong doing—what a testimony. So, they deceived the Medo-Persian King to enact this crazy law. Then they caught Daniel praying to Israel's God and the punishment was a hungry lion's den. The Bible tells us King Darius couldn't sleep all night and in the morning rushed to the potentially gruesome scene. Listen to his words of new-found faith:

Now the king went to his palace and spent the night fasting; and no musicians were brought before him. Also his sleep went from him. Then the king arose very early in the morning and went in haste to the den of lions. And when he came to the den, he cried out with a lamenting voice to Daniel. The king spoke, saying to Daniel, "Daniel, servant of the living God, has your God, whom you serve continually, been able to deliver you from the lions?" (Daniel 6:18–20)

My first question is why was this king so worried about Daniel's fate? And among some good answers I think this is the best one: it is Daniel's righteousness—King Darius understands his complicity in this righteous man's undeserved death sentence, and the Lord is working in the king's heart. He is literally hopeful in Daniel's God and thinking "Just maybe this God of Israel really could save Daniel from the lions." Think of a testimony that would move the most powerful world ruler to think in this repentant and hopeful way! King Darius the Mede is looking for a miracle from the God of Israel! We also consistently see the God given favor Daniel receives from men for his righteous life.

Notice how King Darius characterizes Daniel when calling out to see if he is alive:

> *"Daniel, servant of the living God, has your God, whom you serve continually . . . (Daniel 6:20)*

First what does the King call Daniel? Not only a servant, but whose servant? *The living God's* servant! O help us to see this Lord Jesus, we are here to bring the reality of heaven to a lost and dying people—-the people of the world! That is what our Lord Jesus "was" and "is" trying to tell us:

> *In this manner, therefore, pray: Our Father in heaven, Hallowed be Your name. Your kingdom come. Your will be done On earth as it is in heaven. (Matthew 6:9–10)*

How does His kingdom come and is His will done? On earth through us his obedient servants the same way they obey Him in heaven! Can you imagine those who see our Father and the Lord Jesus today in heaven being preoccupied with things other than His glorious Kingdom and its King? That is how Daniel thought on earth and the mighty King Darius gives witness to this righteous testimony! Another powerful empire's ruler is acknowledging the living God of Israel and this stems from the servant who continually serves the Lord.

> So, the King asks Daniel: *"Daniel, servant of the living God, has your God, whom you serve continually, been able to deliver you from the lions?" (Daniel 6:20)*

The King asks Daniel if this living God that he serves is able to deliver him from the lions. Do you know what the lost want to see today? They want to know if the Lord Jesus is able. If He is able to save Daniel think of what He could do for you and me! "Think of how he then would be able to save me from drugs, a struggling marriage, a broken heart, a horribly difficult life, the troubles of this harsh generation, and ultimately, and most importantly, from my sin!"

All of this is facilitated by what? Daniel lived a righteous life before Darius! This is what untied the Lord's holy hands to move in Daniel's life in such a powerful way. There is something the Lord cannot do—He cannot work many miracles through unbelief and miracle-working faith is directly connected to humble obedience to the Lord.

You remember when our Savior Jesus went to some of those towns that rejected Him. He could have healed, blessed, and even saved them from the grips of sin and hell, but for their unbelief. And be reminded that it is the sin of unbelief that facilitates so much disobedience to the Lord.

"Now He did not do many mighty works there because of their unbelief." (Matthew 13:58)

"For who, having heard, rebelled? Indeed, was it not all who came out of Egypt, led by Moses? Now with whom was He angry forty years? Was it not with those who sinned, whose corpses fell in the wilderness? And to whom did He swear that they would not enter His rest, but to those who did not obey? So we see that they could not enter in because of unbelief." (Hebrews 3:16–19)

But the Holy One of Israel moved mightily through righteous Daniel's testimony so he could answer the King in such a glorious way after the Lord spared him from the lions:

"Then Daniel said to the king, 'O king, live forever! My God sent His angel and shut the lions' mouths, so that they have not hurt me, because I was found innocent before Him; and also, O king, I have done no wrong before you.'" (Daniel 6:21–22)

Look at this response—Daniel is not bitter at the King for having him thrown in the lions' den. Far from it; he sees what the Lord is doing and wants to reach King Darius with His goodness! Don't you see, Daniel completely gave up his rights in his own eyes so He could give glory to the real King—the coming Son of Man! This is downright Christ-like:

> *Let this mind be in you which was also in Christ Jesus, who, being in the form of God, did not consider it robbery to be equal with God, but made Himself of no reputation, taking the form of a bondservant, and coming in the likeness of men. And being found in appearance as a man, He humbled Himself and became obedient to the point of death, even the death of the cross. Therefore God also has highly exalted Him and given Him the name which is above every name, that at the name of Jesus every knee should bow, of those in heaven, and of those on earth, and of those under the earth, and that every tongue should confess that Jesus Christ is Lord, to the glory of God the Father. (Philippians 2:5–11)*

Daniel's life is becoming a type or picture of Messiah Jesus. Daniel was sent to the lion's den by the King. Isaiah 53 tells us that the LORD (Yahweh the Father) was pleased to crush the Son for our sins. Who sentenced the Son of God to die in John 3:16? The Father sent His Only Begotten Son to the lion's den of this world for our sins. The King comes to raise righteous Daniel up from the den and our Holy Father raised righteous Messiah Jesus up from the pit of death and the grave! Daniel's testimony is that he was innocent and our Innocent Sinless Savior did no wrong to God or man. Daniel's life is Christ-like.

Our lives should be Christ-like and we should share the gospel of Jesus Christ with the lost. Some say we should be a silent witness and others boisterously share the gospel without Christ-likeness. But we should live godly lives and share the message of the only way to righteousness—the gospel of Jesus Christ!

"For I am not ashamed of the gospel of Christ, for it is the power of God to salvation for everyone who believes, for the Jew first and also for the Greek. For in it the righteousness of God is revealed from faith to faith; as it is written, 'The just shall live by faith.'" (Romans 1:16–17)

"For our gospel did not come to you in word only, but also in power, and in the Holy Spirit and in much assurance, as you know what kind of men we were among you for your sake." (1 Thessalonians 1:5)

Our lives of righteous words and deeds should bring people to what saves us all—the righteousness of our Heavenly Father in Messiah Jesus His Only Begotten Son! That is exactly what we see from Daniel's life. As we go back to King Darius let's see the fruit of Daniel's righteous faith.

"Now the king was exceedingly glad for him, and commanded that they should take Daniel up out of the den. So Daniel was taken up out of the den, and no injury whatever was found on him, because he believed in his God." (Daniel 6:23)

So, the Lord Jesus is able, just like the Bible tells us:

"Now to Him who is able to do exceedingly abundantly above all that we ask or think, according to the power that works in us, to Him be glory in the church by Christ Jesus to all generations, forever and ever. Amen." (Ephesians 3:20–21)

As we believe in our Lord Jesus, He is able to do exceedingly abundantly above all that we ask or think according to the power that works in us! Is that what most who do not yet believe in Jesus Christ see in His people today? Do they see the power and glory of the Lord Jesus working in and through His church in America?

Sadly, so many professing American Christians today are hooked on the world like a drug addict that needs his daily fix, and the withdrawals will be very painful in the days ahead. There is a carnal movement of professing Christ followers who are looking for the power of God, but really do not love Him. Again, their pursuit of the world gives them away. This is important to remember: The power of the Holy Spirit working in us is for our Father's glory not ours.

Look at what a Christ-like testimony does for a world of lost sinners and the glory they then get to give the Holy God of Israel:

"And the king gave the command, and they brought those men who had accused Daniel, and they cast them into the den of lions—them, their children, and their wives; and the lions overpowered them, and broke all their bones in pieces before they ever came to the bottom of the den." (Daniel 6:24)

Another very important reminder: Vengeance is the Lord's!

Then King Darius wrote: To all peoples, nations, and languages that dwell in all the earth: Peace be multiplied to you. I make a decree that in every dominion of my kingdom men must tremble and fear before the God of Daniel. For He is the living God, And steadfast forever; His kingdom is the one which shall not be destroyed, And His dominion shall endure to the end. He delivers and rescues, And He works signs and wonders In heaven and on earth, Who has delivered Daniel from the power of the lions. So this Daniel prospered in the reign of Darius and in the reign of Cyrus the Persian. (Daniel 6:25–28)

If He is able to save Daniel then Daniel's living God is to be worshiped, followed, trusted, and greatly respected, and shared with the whole world.

Daniel had a testimony that the living God was his God "the God of Daniel" what about you and me?

"And they overcame him by the blood of the Lamb and by the word of their testimony, and they did not love their lives to the death." (Revelation 12:11)

DANIEL'S TESTIMONY REFUGE PRINCIPLES

1) Maintain your testimony!
2) Be sold out for Jesus Christ!
3) Look for His coming!
4) While watching for Him do what He commands you in His word!
5) Love the lost—share the gospel of Jesus Christ!
6) Share the gospel with the lost by word and deed!
7) Be prepared for persecution!
8) Messiah Jesus followers are His humble obedient servants!
9) Develop Kingdom faithfulness!
10) Learn Christ-likeness!

Chapter 15

Daniel's Repentance and Confession

And I prayed to the LORD my God, and made confession . . .
(Daniel 9:4)

*I*n an hour of trouble such as Americans are facing what should be the response of those who desire to be under the protection of the righteousness of Daniel? Mostly what we see today are American Christians tangled up in the Conservative Right of the political system trying to save America by pointing out the sins of all those who do not tow the party line. There are the fiscal Conservatives, social Conservatives, and often times, a combination of the two.

We have learned to shout from the roof tops that lower taxes, smaller government, and fewer regulations will bring our nation back from the edge of the cliff. Or that the primary problem is found in the sins of America like abortion, homosexual marriage, and other grievous offenses. An entire chapter of this book explained how dangerous those sins are to any nation, including the USA. But there is one big problem the "Christian Right" seems to have overlooked that facilitates so much of America's sin. This most often-ignored glaring "pink elephant" at the Evangelical party needs to be identified and dealt with according to the ways of our Lord Jesus! And we can look to righteous Daniel and not only identify it, but also see the only acceptable way it can be addressed from the Lord's perspective.

NOT THE WHITE HOUSE, BUT OUR HOUSE!

The greatest facilitator of America's sin is the sinful American Church Community! We need to see that instead of pointing our finger at all the sins in America and thinking something like this "Get 'em God, they deserve it—give 'em what they been asking for!" we need to see our sins that have turned our nation into a culture dish of darkness! A culture dish is a breeding ground for bacteria and diseases. That is what the lukewarm American Church has facilitated (Revelation 3:14–22) and the lost in our country have no defense for it since they are—*lost*!

Lost is what our Lord Jesus calls those who have not been saved by Him. Once this darkness has consumed our society, and it is almost there, the lost will come for those who should have been salt and light and, through their God-given preserving influence, protected the society from unbridled sin. But instead, so many in the American church have been in love with the world and seem more like citizens of Babylon than Heaven!

Here are some verses that indicate this concept is in the heart of our Lord Jesus:

"You are the salt of the earth; but if the salt loses its flavor, how shall it be seasoned? It is then good for nothing but to be thrown out and trampled underfoot by men." (Matthew 5:13)

"Ye adulterers and adulteresses, know ye not that the friendship of the world is enmity with God? whosoever therefore will be a friend of the world is the enemy of God." (James 4:4, KJV)

"For the time has come for judgment to begin at the house of God; and if it begins with us first, what will be the end of those who do not obey the gospel of God?" (1 Peter 4:17)

The statistics of professing born-again American Christians regarding fornication, adultery, divorce, pornography addiction, impropriety at work, and so on are comparable to those of the non-Christians. While at the same time about two percent share the life-saving gospel with the lost. There is an old quote that goes something like this: "The society Christians refuse to evangelize will one day rise up as their rulers and persecutors." And it may not be long before that is true for professing Christians in America!

What is the righteous answer Daniel gives us for this terribly difficult situation? Think of this scenario: The hard hearted children of Judah were taken into captivity in Babylon. If you read further in Ezekiel chapter 14 it is clear that many of them didn't acknowledge the reason they were no longer in Jerusalem and now residing in Babylon. It was because of this crazy concept that few seem to consider today in American Christian Churches—*their own sin*!

Imagine: for over one hundred years they had been warned by different prophets with the same message—"repent or face judgment!" Like a swerving car on a mountainside with the radio blaring that was piloted by a drunkard, they even careened to a place where they scoffed at the Lord's judgment upon them. They dared the Lord as if somehow they were impervious in their own prideful selves to the strong and mighty hand of the Lord!

But they mocked the messengers of God, despised His words, and scoffed at His prophets, until the wrath of the LORD arose against His people, till there was no remedy. (2 Chronicles 36:16)

Well, today there is certainly no shortage of God mockers in the churches. In the same maddening manner they go on in sin and darkness and almost dare the Lord Jesus to do something about it. In some cases today the drunken driver is the pastor. But as we have seen, Daniel was a man with a different spirit who cooperated with the Holy Spirit of the Lord. And just like then, there are Daniels who will be raised up for the Lord's glory in our hour of judgment! We are going to read the longest passages of scripture that have been placed in this book. May we learn how to respond to the terrible sins of America as we peek into Daniel's prayer closet:

"In the first year of Darius the son of Ahasuerus, of the lineage of the Medes, who was made king over the realm of the Chaldeans—in the first year of his reign I, Daniel, understood by the books the number of the years specified by the word of the LORD

through Jeremiah the prophet, that He would accomplish seventy years in the desolations of Jerusalem." (Daniel 9:1–2)

Daniel understands the season of his people in the timing of the Lord's prophetic word because he reads and knows the word of God and walks closely with the Lord! His prayers are in line with the word of God. Do you think it would be important for us in this season of coming destruction to know and pray according to the word of God?

Then I set my face toward the Lord God to make request by prayer and supplications, with fasting, sackcloth, and ashes. And I prayed to the LORD my God, and made confession, and said, "O Lord, great and awesome God, who keeps His covenant and mercy with those who love Him, and with those who keep His commandments, we have sinned and committed iniquity, we have done wickedly and rebelled, even by departing from Your precepts and Your judgments. Neither have we heeded Your servants the prophets, who spoke in Your name to our kings and our princes, to our fathers and all the people of the land. O Lord, righteousness belongs to You, but to us shame of face, as it is this day—to the men of Judah, to the inhabitants of Jerusalem and all Israel, those near and those far off in all the countries to which You have driven them, because of the unfaithfulness which they have committed against You. (Daniel 9:3–7)

Righteous Daniel identifies their unfaithfulness calling it wicked, rebellious, iniquity, and then places it all in the basket of one word—unfaithfulness, which is another word for adultery. Remember, the Ezekiel passage that states why the judgment is on America is unfaithfulness. Would you prayerfully consider that the unfaithfulness of America is because of the unfaithfulness or adultery of the Church in America against our Lord Jesus Christ—that would be you and me!

Apostle Paul tells us from the Holy Spirit:

"For I am jealous for you with godly jealousy. For I have betrothed you to one husband, that I may present you as a chaste virgin to Christ." (2 Corinthians 11:2)

Before going to approach this Holy Lord righteous Daniel adorns himself with the spiritual and physical garments of humility by fasting and wearing clothes of mourning. We must mourn over our own personal sin and then America's sin—not blame others for it!

"Draw near to God and He will draw near to you. Cleanse your hands, you sinners; and purify your hearts, you double-minded. Lament and mourn and weep! Let your laughter be turned to mourning and your joy to gloom. Humble yourselves in the sight of the Lord, and He will lift you up." (James 4:8–10)

A few paragraphs back we were reminded of how the Children of Israel would not acknowledge their sin that brought on the fury of the Lord. In similar fashion American Christians have been warned for many years of impending judgment. Men and women of the Lord have been shouting "American Christians REPENT before it is too late" for quite some time, and the American Church continues to careen toward Sodom. Before thinking that is a harsh statement, look at what the Lord called the children of Judah as He compared their sins to those of Sodom. This is a verse that was mentioned in an earlier chapter:

"As I live, saith the Lord GOD, Sodom thy sister hath not done, she nor her daughters, as thou hast done, thou and thy daughters. Behold, this was the iniquity of thy sister Sodom, pride, fulness of bread, and abundance of idleness was in her and in her daughters, neither did she strengthen the hand of the poor and needy. And they were haughty, and committed abomination before me: therefore I took them away as I saw good." (Ezekiel 16:48–50, KJV)

You see, pride and all these other sins, that too often fit American Christianity to the letter, "sowed" by the wickedness of Judah, who were also called the people of God, progressed into or "reaped" in Israel the unbridled sin of Sodom! Judah ended up in the same kind of condition as Sodom by the time the Lord judged them. The sins of the church in America have facilitated a dark environment that has produced abortion and other violent crimes, the drug epidemic, the fornication movement including exploding homosexual expansion, and a growing anti-Israel climate. Our sins in the American Church have created an environment that has produced the BIG THREE!

Like Daniel cried out, how shameful our sin is before our Heavenly Father and the lost of America. May we see the righteous way forward and learn from our righteous brother Daniel.

> *O Lord, to us belongs shame of face, to our kings, our princes, and our fathers, because we have sinned against You. To the Lord our God belong mercy and forgiveness, though we have rebelled against Him. We have not obeyed the voice of the LORD our God, to walk in His laws, which He set before us by His servants the prophets. Yes, all Israel has transgressed Your law, and has departed so as not to obey Your voice; therefore the curse and the oath written in the Law of Moses the servant of God have been poured out on us, because we have sinned against Him. And He has confirmed His words, which He spoke against us and against our judges who judged us, by bringing upon us a great disaster; for under the whole heaven such has never been done as what has been done to Jerusalem. (Daniel 9:8–12)*

The Curse and the Oath in The Law

In Daniel's prayer he is identifying the Lord's righteous standard found many places in the Law (Torah)— first five books of Moses. Unlike most from Judah, Daniel is acknowledging Judah's sins.

> *"But if you do not obey Me, and do not observe all these commandments, and if you despise My statutes, or if your soul abhors My judgments, so that you do not perform all My commandments, but break My covenant, I also will do this to you: I will even appoint terror over you, wasting disease and fever which shall consume the eyes and cause sorrow of heart. And you shall sow your seed in vain, for your enemies shall eat it. I will set My face against you, and you shall be defeated by your*

enemies. Those who hate you shall reign over you, and you shall flee when no one pursues you." (Leviticus 26:14–17)

It must be noted that today, we are not under the Law (Galatians 5:18), nor are born-again believers in Jesus under the Father's wrath. Yet, many in American Churches today have never been born from above and remain in great peril. And in the same way that Daniel confessed his sin and acknowledged the warnings of judgment that were disregarded, we need to humbly do the same. And as we have seen, there are plenty of New Covenant passages, pertaining to the fear of God for those who are born again, that we have blown through with total disregard. Here is another important series of warnings from our Savior:

"Enter by the narrow gate; for wide is the gate and broad is the way that leads to destruction, and there are many who go in by it. Because narrow is the gate and difficult is the way which leads to life, and there are few who find it." (Matthew 7:13–14)

"Not everyone who says to Me, 'Lord, Lord,' shall enter the kingdom of heaven, but he who does the will of My Father in heaven. Many will say to Me in that day, 'Lord, Lord, have we not prophesied in Your name, cast out demons in Your name, and done many wonders in Your name?' And then I will declare to them, 'I never knew you; depart from Me, you who practice lawlessness!'" (Matthew 7:21–23)

We have it all backwards, we have a Christianity that looks like the wide road that leads to destruction—not the narrow one that leads to life!

Daniel's Righteous Intercession

Why would a righteous man like Daniel who was not guilty of the same sins as most of his people pray for those who had been so wicked? What we will find in these precious passages of life is that Daniel understood he too needed grace and mercy. He did not place himself above those who had lived in iniquity, and Daniel understood the only way out was grace and mercy from the Law-giver.

Additionally, Daniel associated himself with the sins of his people that he might intercede for them in hopes that many would be spared from wrath. It is the opposite of "Get 'em God!" We can look at the mercy that Daniel knew to be available from the Torah and see that his prayer is one the Lord must honor because it is according to His word!

But if they confess their iniquity and the iniquity of their fathers, with their unfaithfulness in which they were unfaithful to Me, and that they also have walked contrary to Me, and that I also have walked contrary to them and have brought them into the land of their enemies; if their uncircumcised hearts are humbled, and they accept their guilt—then I will remember My covenant with Jacob, and My covenant with Isaac and My covenant with Abraham I will remember; I will remember the land. The land also shall be left empty by them, and will enjoy its sabbaths while it lies desolate without them; they will accept their guilt, because they despised My judgments and because their soul abhorred My statutes. Yet for all that, when they are in the land of their enemies, I will not cast them away, nor shall I abhor them, to utterly destroy them and break My covenant with them; for I am the LORD their God. (Leviticus 26:40–44)

The Iniquity of Our Fathers

The passing down of iniquities of the fathers has at least a couple of meanings, both of which I will briefly discuss from this Leviticus passage. There is a truth about fathers passing sins down that are inherited by their genetic fathers. And to some degree it applies here. Additionally, there are generations of American church movements, leaders, and churches going back to the early 1900s in America who have handed down a lukewarm and "gospel-light" version of the truth. There are also modern church movements, leaders, and churches that are facilitating dark and demonic environments which are making professing Evangelical Christians less relevant to our dying nation with every moment that passes!

We must repent of and confess as sin these things, and more as the Holy Spirit leads, handed down from previous generations:

- Pride.
- Gluttony.
- Lack of compassion for the lost.
- Idleness—lack of Kingdom advancing activity (authentic worship, sharing the gospel, prayer, etc.).
- A social gospel that replaces the gospel of Jesus Christ with doing humanitarian and charitable deeds.
- Minimizing the deadliness of sin.
- The lack of fear of God.
- Lust of the flesh, lust of the eyes, the pride of life—worldliness.
- Lack of compassion for the poor, orphans, widows.
- Lack of concern for Israel.

The Holy One of Israel is the God of covenant. The covenants He made with Abraham, Isaac, and Jacob are fully realized in the gospel of Jesus Christ (Galatians 3:8). Our Abba's covenants provide mercy and grace for those who will repent or turn from their iniquity (known flagrant wickedness). Daniel understood this from Leviticus and was seeking the Lord's prescribed mercy not only for himself, but also for his people! What love—what unselfishness—what Christ-likeness.

As it is written in the Law of Moses, all this disaster has come upon us; yet we have not made our prayer before the LORD our God, that we might turn from our iniquities and understand Your truth. Therefore the LORD has kept the disaster in mind, and brought it upon us; for the LORD our God is righteous in all the works which He does, though we have not obeyed His voice. And now, O Lord our God, who brought Your people out of the land of Egypt with a mighty hand, and made Yourself a name, as it is this day—we have sinned, we have done wickedly! (Daniel 9:13–15)

Daniel fully agrees with the Lord that His judgment is just and appropriate. He agrees with His righteous judgments and again lays the blame where few would—on the covenant people of God who are supposed to be salt and light. Covenant believers in the God of Jacob are required by God to reflect His righteousness! Thankfully, in His righteousness there is mercy and grace in repentance of iniquity.

O Lord, according to all Your righteousness, I pray, let Your anger and Your fury be turned away from Your city Jerusalem, Your holy mountain; because for our sins, and for the iniquities of our fathers, Jerusalem and Your people are a reproach to all those around us. Now therefore, our God, hear the prayer of Your servant, and his supplications, and for the Lord's sake cause Your face to shine on Your sanctuary, which is desolate. O my God, incline Your ear and hear; open Your eyes and see our desolations, and the city which is called by Your name; for we do not present our supplications before You because of our righteous deeds, but because of Your great mercies. O Lord, hear! O Lord, forgive! O Lord, listen and act! Do not delay for Your own sake, my God, for Your city and Your people are called by Your name. (Daniel 9:16–19)

What did the Lord do in response to Daniel's righteous response to Judah's sin? And just in case we have forgotten look at the relationship here between Daniel and His God. He knows and is known by the Lord! This is not dead religion but a relationship of love between Father and son. We are adopted sons in Christ Jesus!

"For as many as are led by the Spirit of God, these are sons of God." (Romans 8:14)

The Lord Answers Righteous Daniel

Now while I was speaking, praying, and confessing my sin and the sin of my people Israel, and presenting my supplication before the LORD my God for the holy mountain of my God, yes, while I was speaking in prayer, the man Gabriel, whom I had seen in the vision at the beginning, being caused to fly swiftly, reached me about the time of the evening offering. And he informed me, and talked with me, and said, "O Daniel, I have now come forth to give you skill to understand. At the beginning of your supplications the command went out, and I have come to tell you, for you are greatly beloved; therefore consider the matter, and understand the vision . . . (Daniel 9:20–23)

The first Daniel chapter of this book started off with the words *"Oh Daniel, man greatly beloved"* from Daniel 10:10. Yet look here in Daniel 9 at the economy of the Lord for the man of God as he speaks, prays, and confesses his and Israel's sin. This wonderful Father in heaven sends His messenger to Daniel at the time he is praying. Actually, the angel goes on to deliver to Daniel one of the most powerful prophecies ever given to mankind. This prophecy would span thousands of years and includes:

- The Jews sent back to rebuild Jerusalem (Daniel 9:25)
- First coming of Messiah Jesus (Daniel 9:25)
- Crucifixion of Messiah Jesus (Daniel 9:26)
- Destruction of Jerusalem and the temple in Jerusalem by Romans (Daniel 9:26)
- The anti-Christ from Rome (Daniel 9:26)
- Great world trouble (Daniel 9:26)
- Great seven year tribulation (Daniel 9:27)
- The abomination of desolation of anti-Christ (Daniel 9:27, Matthew 24:15, 2 Thessalonians 2:1–4)
- And of course in Daniel 2:7 and other places in the book named after him he receives amazing prophecies including, but not limited to, major kingdoms that would rule the earth and the second coming of Messiah Jesus to reign over the universe from Jerusalem!

Today for His people who will love our Lord Jesus with all their heart and love their neighbor as themselves He will fill them with the Holy Spirit! For those who will turn from their wickedness, pray without ceasing, confess their sins along with those of America they will hear from the Holy One of Israel Jesus Christ by the Holy Spirit and give glory to our Father in heaven! They will walk under the protection of the righteousness of Daniel during the time of Ezekiel's judgment on America.

DANIEL'S REPENTANCE AND CONFESSION REFUGE POINTS

1) Know the word of God and pray accordingly!
2) Do not trust in the world's political system to save America!
3) Do not blame the lost for America's trouble!
4) Take personal ownership for the sins of the American Christian environment!
5) Repent—turn away from iniquity including lukewarmness!
6) Confess personal sin and the sins of America to our Lord Jesus Christ!
7) Agree with the Lord that His judgment is righteous and appropriate!
8) Hear from our Lord Jesus and receive His love and forgiveness!
9) Tell others what He tells you!
10) Learn to fast and pray regularly!

Chapter 16

Righteousness Like Job

You have heard of the perseverance of Job . . . (James 5:11)

J ob's life was so important and the righteousness of Job is identified in the New Testament book of James with the words—
patient perseverance!

It is only grace through faith that brings a man or woman with
a natural sin nature to a place where they can trust our Lord Jesus
and persevere through tragic ongoing catastrophes such as Job's.
Yet, in the midst of these intense difficulties, as we see in Job's life,
our faithful Savior Jesus is with us and one day will fully restore us
more than we can imagine!

The Bible's initial account of Job is that he was a righteous man.
His happy life fit into the mindset of modern American Christianity at
the beginning of the story. Not only was he a blameless God-fearing
man, but he was blessed with a healthy family and great possessions.
He was a great man recognized as such by all in his region.

> *"There was a man in the land of Uz, whose name was Job; and
> that man was blameless and upright, and one who feared God
> and shunned evil. And seven sons and three daughters were
> born to him. Also, his possessions were seven thousand sheep,
> three thousand camels, five hundred yoke of oxen, five hundred*

female donkeys, and a very large household, so that this man was the greatest of all the people of the East." (Job 1:1–3)

This is where the trouble begins—not only in Job's life but in the American Christian's interpretation of his trouble. I say that because as Job's life is tragically turned upside down the modern American Christian "spins" attempt to keep the modern doctrines intact and to do so has to tamper with the Bible. But wouldn't it be better to keep the Bible intact and instead change our ways? His word is unchangeable, no matter how man tries to tamper with it!

Now there was a day when the sons of God came to present themselves before the LORD, and Satan also came among them. And the LORD said to Satan, "From where do you come?" So Satan answered the LORD and said, "From going to and fro on the earth, and from walking back and forth on it." Then the LORD said to Satan, "Have you considered My servant Job, that there is none like him on the earth, a blameless and upright man, one who fears God and shuns evil?" (Job 1:6–8)

I have heard people say that it was Job's sin, or that the devil came looking for Job, and the devil is the one who brought all his soon coming suffering. But actually, if we will just look at the Bible, it clearly tells us that the Lord brings Job to Satan's attention and tells him that Job is the Lord's uniquely blameless and upright servant. Who brings the trouble to Job's life? We will see even more clearly by the end of the account of Job that it is the Lord.

So Satan answered the LORD and said, "Does Job fear God for nothing? Have You not made a hedge around him, around his household, and around all that he has on every side? You have blessed the work of his hands, and his possessions have increased in the land. But now, stretch out Your hand and touch all that he has, and he will surely curse You to Your face!" And the LORD said to Satan, "Behold, all that he has is in your power; only do not lay a hand on his person." So Satan went out from the presence of the LORD. (Job 1:9–12)

After challenging Satan, by bringing Job to his attention, the Lord gives the devil permission, with boundaries, to test Job to see if he will curse the Lord. Think of this—the devil wants people who profess to follow Jesus to curse our Savior. And also consider, if someone will curse our Savior there is something wrong with their faith that needs adjusting. That is not to say that Job didn't question the Lord and outwardly grieve over his loss and suffering. Yet this is miles apart from cursing the Lord. You see, this is a heavenly test for Job. Faith in the Lord Jesus is not authentic if it is not tested.

Here It Comes

"Now there was a day when his sons and daughters were eating and drinking wine in their oldest brother's house; and a messenger came to Job and said, "The oxen were plowing and the donkeys feeding beside them, when the Sabeans raided them and took them away—indeed they have killed the servants with the edge of the sword; and I alone have escaped to tell you!" (Job 1:13–15)

More Sorrow

While he was still speaking, another also came and said, "The fire of God fell from heaven and burned up the sheep and the servants, and consumed them; and I alone have escaped to tell you!" While he was still speaking, another also came and said, "The Chaldeans formed three bands, raided the camels and took them away, yes, and killed the servants with the edge of the sword; and I alone have escaped to tell you!" (Job 1:16–17)

The Unthinkable—Losing All His Children for Whom Job Faithfully Prayed!

And his sons would go and feast in their houses, each on his appointed day, and would send and invite their three sisters to eat and drink with them. So it was, when the days of feasting had run their course, that Job would send and sanctify them, and he would rise early in the morning and offer burnt offerings according to the number of them all. For Job said, "It may be that my sons have sinned and cursed God in their hearts." Thus Job did regularly. (Job 1:4–5)

"While he was still speaking, another also came and said, 'Your sons and daughters were eating and drinking wine in their oldest brother's house, and suddenly a great wind came from across the wilderness and struck the four corners of the house, and it fell on the young people, and they are dead; and I alone have escaped to tell you!'" (Job 1:18–19)

The Righteous Response

What was Job's response? How many scenarios go through the natural mind under duress from any one of these tragedies? But after all this and then losing his precious children for whom Job regularly prayed—would he curse the Lord? I am so thankful for this man of God and the example of his righteous response:

Then Job arose, tore his robe, and shaved his head; and he fell to the ground and worshiped. And he said: "Naked I came from my mother's womb, And naked shall I return there. The LORD gave, and the LORD has taken away; Blessed be the name of the LORD." In all this Job did not sin nor charge God with wrong. (Job 1:20–22)

Job is responding with his righteous life as an authentic follower of the Lord. It is when the most unbearable trouble comes that the truth about us is revealed. Beyond the natural, only authentic faith can operate in someone's life to empower the response of authentic worship to such painful trauma. Job did not charge the Lord with wrong because he knows in his innermost being that He would never do wrong. But isn't it wrong for the Lord to bring all this trouble into Job's life? You can hear again Job's answer to that question:

"Naked I came from my mother's womb, And naked shall I return there. The LORD gave, and the LORD has taken away; Blessed be the name of the LORD." (Job 1:21)

This is an expression of pure worship—the kind that our Savior Jesus mentions to the Samaritan woman:

"But the hour is coming, and now is, when the true worshipers will worship the Father in spirit and truth; for the Father is seeking such to worship Him." (John 4:23)

I am so very thankful for this man's example, for had I never seen it, I don't know how I would have responded to my most recent painful trauma. My mother was the first one to lead me to Messiah Jesus. She lived a life of prayer and unique love for our Messiah. She walked by faith even moving to Israel in the early 1980s with little money or provisions. At the age of sixty-seven, cancer returned to her body from twenty years earlier.

Almost immediately after hearing how bad it was, through indescribable heartache, I got down on my knees and said this to the Lord: "If Job could say these words, then I can say them," and I quoted Job's words upon hearing about his great loss. However, maybe there would be healing for my precious mother.

I fasted, prayed, and spoke the Lords' words back to Him from the Bible about healing. As she got worse, I refused to listen to the doctors—hey I had seen the Lord heal people in Africa of life threatening things, including HIV. Then I had to face that the Lord was taking my mother—this time there wouldn't be healing. Yet there "with me" was my Immanuel (God with us) Savior Jesus! The reality of these verses became like solid ground under my feet and in my heart:

But I do not want you to be ignorant, brethren, concerning those who have fallen asleep, lest you sorrow as others who have no hope. For if we believe that Jesus died and rose again, even so God will bring with Him those who sleep in Jesus. For this we say to you by the word of the Lord, that we who are alive and remain until the coming of the Lord will by no means precede those who are asleep. For the Lord Himself will descend from heaven with a shout, with the voice of an archangel, and with the trumpet of God. And the dead in Christ will rise first. Then we who are alive and remain shall be caught up together with them in the clouds to meet the Lord in the air. And thus we shall always be with the Lord. Therefore comfort one another with these words. (1 Thessalonians 4:13–18)

You see, these things are not natural. To respond to tragedy with authentic worship doesn't make the pain go away. No, but it gives our Father in heaven freedom to comfort us and invites the Savior into the operating room of our lives. It is in these times of suffering that He changes us into His image.

An obvious question is, "Why this painful process?" It is when we are this shattered that a true follower of our Lord Jesus Christ is most closely associated with His ministry on earth. So many do not see the value of this important principle, and here is the reason. Most American Christians have never considered that in the same way our Savior came to save the lost and be a witness to the truth, we are here to finish the work. Our Lord Jesus has left us here for our earthly ministry (Acts 1:8). When we receive our earthly ministry being associated with His ministry becomes an honor and an example of how to live.

It is also true that by the tests He brings into our lives we are made to understand how completely reliant we are upon Him and not on ourselves. In James 1:2–4 the word *patience* in the original Biblical Greek language is also interchangeable with the word *endurance.*

"My brethren, count it all joy when you fall into various trials, knowing that the testing of your faith produces patience. But let patience have its perfect work, that you may be perfect (mature) and complete, lacking nothing." (James 1:2–4)

Therefore, having been justified by faith, we have peace with God through our Lord Jesus Christ, through whom also we have access by faith into this grace in which we stand, and rejoice in hope of the glory of God. And not only that, but we also glory in tribulations, knowing that tribulation produces persever-ance; and perseverance, character; and character, hope. Now hope does not disappoint, because the love of God has been poured out in our hearts by the Holy Spirit who was given to us. (Romans 5:1–5)

The Apostle Paul had given up everything to follow our Lord Jesus. Our Messiah had turned his entire life upside down which is good because Paul's entire life was in direct opposition to our Savior. Paul considered the loss of all his life's work this way:

Yet indeed I also count all things loss for the excellence of the knowledge of Christ Jesus my Lord, for whom I have suffered the loss of all things, and count them as rubbish, that I may gain Christ and be found in Him, not having my own righteousness, which is from the law, but that which is through faith in Christ, the righteousness which is from God by faith . . . (Philippians 3:8–9)

The Apostle Paul wanted us to understand the great honor granted to us that we could suffer in the name of our Lord Jesus Christ. Consider Paul's words, written from prison, regarding his desire to be associated in every way with our Lord:

"For to you it has been granted on behalf of Christ, not only to believe in Him, but also to suffer for His sake, having the same conflict which you saw in me and now hear is in me." (Philippians 1:29–30)

". . . that I may know Him and the power of His resurrection, and the fellowship of His sufferings, being conformed to His death, if, by any means, I may attain to the resurrection from the dead." (Philippians 3:10–11)

It is as we are conformed to the crucifixion of Christ through great trials that we truly can live! So many Christians would tell us they want the power of His resurrection, but it only comes along with the fellowship of His sufferings!

Then Jesus said to His disciples, "If anyone desires to come after Me, let him deny himself, and take up his cross, and follow Me. For whoever desires to save his life will lose it, but whoever loses his life for My sake will find it. For what profit is it to a man if he gains the whole world, and loses his own soul? Or what will a man give in exchange for his soul? (Matthew 16:24–26)

How foreign the life of the cross is to American Christianity! How strange this walk with Jesus is to most Americans professing to be evangelical saints. Oh Lord Jesus please restore to us the power of the cross!

A man like Job cannot lose! Do you want to know why? It is summed up in a saying a dear pastor friend of mine told me. It goes something like this: "The best way to beat your enemies is to outlast them!" The patient endurance the Lord gives us in trials makes us strong enough to outlast our enemies: the flesh, the world system set against Christ, and the devil and people motivated by them against us.

"By your patience possess your souls." (Luke 21:19)

JOB'S PERSEVERANCE REFUGE PRINCIPLES

1) Consider trials as from our Lord Jesus.
2) Trials test our faith in our Lord Jesus.
3) Satan wants us to distrust our Savior.
4) Respond to trials with authentic worship.
5) Identify with the sufferings of Messiah Jesus.
6) Receive comfort from the Lord.
7) Place your hope fully in our Lord Jesus!

Chapter 17

Job's Righteousness — The Rest of the Story

. . . that the Lord is very compassionate and merciful.
(James 5:11)

*A*s we continue to observe the life of Job, first we will see that his suffering was not yet over after learning of the loss of his children—it had just begun. Yet we will also see with all the ups and downs, lefts and rights, the Lord's plan is one of redemption and restoration for Job. His plan from the beginning is to restore Job fully and bring him closer to the Lord. Consider the most important thing in life is to be closer to Him!

> *"Then the LORD said to Satan, "Have you considered My servant Job, that there is none like him on the earth, a blameless and upright man, one who fears God and shuns evil? And still he holds fast to his integrity, although you incited Me against him, to destroy him without cause." (Job 2:3)*

Again, we see the Lord challenging Satan and egging him on to further stretch Job. If He does this with Job, could He do this with you and me? If so, what can we learn, and how can this help us in the coming days? These are important questions, and thankfully there is good news for those who persevere.

So Satan answered the LORD and said, "Skin for skin! Yes, all that a man has he will give for his life. But stretch out Your hand now, and touch his bone and his flesh, and he will surely curse You to Your face!" And the LORD said to Satan, "Behold, he is in your hand, but spare his life." So Satan went out from the presence of the LORD, and struck Job with painful boils from the sole of his foot to the crown of his head. And he took for himself a potsherd with which to scrape himself while he sat in the midst of the ashes. (Job 2:4–8)

Job's Wife and Three Friends

So, after losing almost everything including his children now Job is tormented on and in his body day and night! It is in this time that surely the Lord would raise up his godly wife to stand with Job in faith and prayer—right?

"Then his wife said to him, 'Do you still hold fast to your integrity? Curse God and die!'" (Job 2:9)

Job's test is intensifying still in that his wife is now cursing the Lord and not only must he be strong for himself, but also for his precious wife who may be so grief stricken that she is at the end of her faith. The Bible is not clear about this, but one thing we do know, Job has someone in his home to join in cursing God with if that is in his heart. Yet, his faith continues to cause Job to persevere:

"But he said to her, 'You speak as one of the foolish women speaks. Shall we indeed accept good from God, and shall we not accept adversity?' In all this Job did not sin with his lips." (Job 2:10)

Amazing grace operates through amazing faith! Job in all his suffering will not allow his wife to speak against the Lord even in the midst of such suffering. He acknowledges it is the Lord who brings the good and the bad. What great faith—to understand and acknowledge that the good times and the difficult times all come from the Lord and to receive one, we must accept the other. Also, after all that the Father in heaven, Savior Jesus, and Holy Spirit does for us every day, thanklessness is too often what He receives from us. Job has an incredible perspective especially given his circumstances.

To complete the circle of suffering Job had three friends. When they arrived on the scene to comfort Job they brought clubs and brass knuckles instead of love and mercy. You know the old saying "Christians often times bury their wounded." They spoke wrongly about the Lord in this situation and even accused Job of wickedness:

> *"Now when Job's three friends heard of all this adversity that had come upon him, each one came from his own place—Eliphaz the Temanite, Bildad the Shuhite, and Zophar the Naamathite." (Job 2:11)*

> *Eliphaz: "Behold, happy is the man whom God corrects; Therefore do not despise the chastening of the Almighty. (Job 5:17)*

> *Bildad: "If your sons have sinned against Him, He has cast them away for their transgression." (Job 8:4)*

> *Zophar: "If you would prepare your heart, And stretch out your hands toward Him; If iniquity were in your hand, and you put it far away, And would not let wickedness dwell in your tents; Then surely you could lift up your face without spot; Yes, you could be steadfast, and not fear; Because you would forget your misery, And remember it as waters that have passed away, And your life would be brighter than noonday. (Job 11:13–17)*

While Job is suffering miserably, the first friend speaks of Job's need to be happy in correction, the second tells Job that his children got what they deserved, and the third told Job he was wicked and needed to repent. Job hits the nail on the head and calls all three "miserable comforters," which is certainly true. In the book of Job during their entire discourse toward their agonizing friend these guys said things that may have had elements of truth, but theirs were not the right words at the right time. They were rebuked later by the Lord for not accurately representing Him toward Job. Often, it is not only what we say, but the spirit in which we say it. We can benefit from these words from Paul:

> *"Rejoice with those who rejoice, and weep with those who weep." (Romans 12:15)*

Job's Righteous Sayings In Response To His Friends

> *"Though He slay me, yet will I trust Him." (Job 13:15a)*

> *"But He knows the way that I take; When He has tested me, I shall come forth as gold." (Job 23:10)*

> *"I have made a covenant with my eyes; Why then should I look upon a young woman?" (Job 31:1)*

> *"For I know that my Redeemer lives, And He shall stand at last on the earth . . ." (Job 19:25)*

As this crisis continues, we can be reminded that even in Job's righteous life there are deep places in his soul where he needs repentance, confession of sin, cleansing, and adjustments. As Job gets to the end of his faith, which is where trials often lead us, the root of a spiritual problem is revealed. He begins to justify himself, and none of us is righteous in and of himself. A young man who came with Job's three friends hears this and identifies the problem. Interestingly, Job and his three friends were rebuked by the Lord, but not Elihu as he discerned the matter correctly:

> *"So these three men ceased answering Job, because he was righteous in his own eyes. Then the wrath of Elihu, the son of Barachel the Buzite, of the family of Ram, was aroused against Job; his wrath was aroused because he justified himself rather than God. Also against his three friends his wrath was aroused,*

because they had found no answer, and yet had condemned Job." (Job 32:1–3)

Then the LORD answered Job out of the whirlwind, and said: "Who is this who darkens counsel By words without knowledge? Now prepare yourself like a man; I will question you, and you shall answer Me." Where were you when I laid the foundations of the earth? Tell Me, if you have understanding. Who determined its measurements? Surely you know! Or who stretched the line upon it? To what were its foundations fastened? Or who laid its cornerstone, When the morning stars sang together, And all the sons of God shouted for joy?" (Job 38:1–7)

This is a small snapshot of the Lord's explanation to Job of the term "the Potter and the clay" and which one of the two we are compared to the Lord. His response to Job shows us that even in a life set on righteousness we have sin within us and that even in suffering our Heavenly Father knows best. The first epistle (letter) of John in the New Testament reminds us well:

"If we say that we have no sin, we deceive ourselves, and the truth is not in us. If we confess our sins, He is faithful and just to forgive us our sins and to cleanse us from all unrighteousness." (1 John 1:8–9)

Job heard from the Lord and was brought to a place of brokenness and humility before Him with no defense left of himself. Instead of asking anymore questions and defending himself Job realized something that makes our pain diminish greatly—the glory and majesty of our Lord Jesus! Job totally flung Himself to the mercy of the Lord. That is the best place to be, for in Him we find grace and mercy:

"Moreover the LORD answered Job, and said: 'Shall the one who contends with the Almighty correct Him? He who rebukes God, let him answer it.' Then Job answered the LORD and said: 'Behold, I am vile; What shall I answer You? I lay my hand over my mouth. Once I

have spoken, but I will not answer; Yes, twice, but I will proceed no further.'" (Job 40:1–5)

Then later in chapter 42:

Then Job answered the LORD and said: "I know that You can do everything, And that no purpose of Yours can be withheld from You. You asked, 'Who is this who hides counsel without knowledge?' Therefore I have uttered what I did not understand, Things too wonderful for me, which I did not know. Listen, please, and let me speak; You said, 'I will question you, and you shall answer Me.' "I have heard of You by the hearing of the ear, But now my eye sees You. Therefore I abhor myself, And repent in dust and ashes." (Job 42:1–6)

It is when we get to a place, by Revelation of the Holy Spirit, of seeing our Lord Jesus for who He is—the KING of kings and Lord of lords that we respond in this way. There are times when it takes unimaginable trials to bring us to this place and dear ones (this will be hard to hear,) the average prideful, arrogant, American Christian needs to see who our Lord Jesus is today! Regarding these difficult to hear descriptions of ourselves, I will be the first to say that at times they have described me. Guilty as charged, yet forgiven by the Lamb of God who takes away the sins of the world!

"But He gives more grace. Therefore He says: 'God resists the proud, But gives grace to the humble.'" (James 4:6)

"Humble yourselves in the sight of the Lord, and He will lift you up." (James 4:10)

"For thus says the High and Lofty One Who inhabits eternity, whose name is Holy: 'I dwell in the high and holy place, With him who has a contrite and humble spirit, To revive the spirit of the humble, And to revive the heart of the contrite ones.'" (Isaiah 57:15)

It is when we are humble, broken, and contrite that the Lord will lift us up and restore us! This is where we can have fellowship with Him and one another. Why is the American Church so fractured and free of close relationships within the church body? Why is revival, and our desperate need for it, so foreign? In a word—pride. In another two words it is "self-reliance." But our Father draws near to the humble. Our Father dwells with and revives those who honor Him for who He is as they truly want to be near to Him. Oh, I want to be near to my Father in heaven—I want to be humble before Him!

Job's Restoration!

We earthbound children of God (if you are born again as in John 3:3) need to remember that our Savior Jesus is in the restoration business! There is a wonderful song that says "It will be worth it all when we see Jesus." Job's loss and suffering were all temporary. Yet the redemptive work the Lord was doing in Job, his wife, his three friends (Job 42:1–9), and even his children, and others who lost their lives in the Lord in this process, can only be measured by eternity!

Let's see the wonderful earthly restoration of Job and then look at our eternal restoration.

> And so it was, after the LORD had spoken these words to Job, that the LORD said to Eliphaz the Temanite, "My wrath is aroused against you and your two friends, for you have not spoken of Me what is right, as My servant Job has. Now therefore, take for yourselves seven bulls and seven rams, go to My servant Job, and offer up for yourselves a burnt offering; and My servant Job shall pray for you. For I will accept him, lest I deal with you according to your folly; because you have not spoken of Me what is right, as My servant Job has." (Job 42:7–8)

There is a powerfully true old saying: "It all comes out in the wash." While these three friends of Job were heaping it on him, Job had little recourse. But it all came out in the wash that their treatment of this suffering brother in the Lord was wrong. To be released from their sin, they had to get right with the Lord and then with Job. Then, Job had to forgive them by offering up an authentic prayer for his friends to the Lord. Agreement with the Lord over our sin, receiving cleansing and forgiveness, going to an offended brother, and the offended brother forgiving the offender are all pleasing things to the Lord and bring great restoration:

> *"So Eliphaz the Temanite and Bildad the Shuhite and Zophar the Naamathite went and did as the LORD commanded them; for the LORD had accepted Job. And the LORD restored Job's losses when he prayed for his friends. Indeed the LORD gave Job twice as much as he had before." (Job 42:9–10)*

There is a technique green thumbs know about called "pruning." Thankfully, our Father in heaven has quite a knack for growing up healthy disciples of Jesus Christ. He uses pruning to cut us back so that we do not grow into something that doesn't resemble our Lord Jesus. But instead, though it can be very painful, we grow into much stronger and more vibrant followers who are true witnesses of the Lord:

> *"I am the true vine, and My Father is the vinedresser. Every branch in Me that does not bear fruit He takes away; and every branch that bears fruit He prunes, that it may bear more fruit." (John 15:1–2)*

When the Lord restores, He sure does it right! We will look at a passage that itemizes some of the restoration along with other verses upon which we can stand in the days ahead. Remember, these days of judgment are upon us, and I believe, from what we have seen together in the Bible, they will get more difficult soon. Also notice in this passage that the Bible teaches clearly that the Lord brought this adversity to Job.

> *Then all his brothers, all his sisters, and all those who had been his acquaintances before, came to him and ate food with him in his house; and they consoled him and comforted him for all*

the adversity that the LORD had brought upon him. Each one gave him a piece of silver and each a ring of gold. Now the LORD blessed the latter days of Job more than his beginning; for he had fourteen thousand sheep, six thousand camels, one thousand yoke of oxen, and one thousand female donkeys. He also had seven sons and three daughters. (Job 42:11–13)

The Bible goes on to say that Job lived to a ripe old age, that his children were the best looking in all the land, and that he was blessed beyond measure the rest of his life. You see, his was a season of affliction. And in the life of those made righteous by Jesus Christ there are many seasons of affliction. A season of great affliction is coming to America. May we be comforted by these verses of scripture:

"He delivers the poor in their affliction, And opens their ears in oppression." (Job 36:15)

"Look on my affliction and my pain, And forgive all my sins." (Psalm 25:18)

"Many are the afflictions of the righteous, But the LORD delivers him out of them all." (Psalm 34:19)

"This is my comfort in my affliction, For Your word has given me life." (119:50)

"For He healed many, so that as many as had afflictions pressed about Him to touch Him." (Mark 3:10)

"For our light affliction, which is but for a moment, is working for us a far more exceeding and eternal weight of glory . . ." (2 Corinthians 4:17)

"But you be watchful in all things, endure afflictions, do the work of an evangelist, fulfill your ministry." (2 Timothy 4:5)

Eternal Restoration!

The restoration the Lord gave Job on earth is just the beginning not to be compared with the endless restoration in the next life! And for some special saints restoration doesn't come in this life but is certainly reserved with special rewards in the next. The scriptures speak for themselves and the Holy Spirit gives us a glimpse of the soon coming excitement of the glory of our eternal life in Jesus Christ! It truly will be worth it all when we see Jesus:

"For I consider that the sufferings of this present time are not worthy to be compared with the glory which shall be revealed in us." (Romans 8:18)

"Beloved, now we are children of God; and it has not yet been revealed what we shall be, but we know that when He is revealed, we shall be like Him, for we shall see Him as He is." (1 John 3:2)

"But as it is written: 'Eye has not seen, nor ear heard, Nor have entered into the heart of man The things which God has prepared for those who love Him.' But God has revealed them to us through His Spirit." (1 Corinthians 2:9–10)

"And God will wipe away every tear from their eyes; there shall be no more death, nor sorrow, nor crying. There shall be no more pain, for the former things have passed away." (Revelation 21:4)

JOB'S RESTORATION PRINCIPLES

1) Get things right with the Lord Jesus.
2) Ask forgiveness from those you have offended.
3) Humility and brokenness please the Lord.
4) Draw near to Abba Father and He will draw near to you!
5) The righteous have many afflictions.
6) The Lord delivers Him out of them all!
7) Restoration will come in this life and/or the next!
8) It will be worth it all when we see our Lord Jesus!

Chapter 18

The Days of Noah – And the Gospel of Jesus Christ

But as the days of Noah were, so also will the coming of the Son of Man be. (Matthew 24:37)

*I*n conclusion of all we have seen in *America's Ark* there are important questions and answers that are the most critical for this moment in time:

Is The Lord Jesus Christ Returning Soon?

Today people mock, scorn, and laugh at the term "Noah's Ark" or "Noah's Flood." They laughed in Noah's day too, but look at what the Lord Jesus Christ said that was quoted by the New Testament author Luke:

"They ate, they drank, they married wives, they were given in marriage, until the day that Noah entered the ark, and the flood came and destroyed them all." (Luke 17:27)

They were laughing as Noah built that ark and mocked him all the way—until it started raining and flooding and they were all destroyed. In the same way people will be mocking those who truly seek after the righteousness of Noah, Daniel, and Job today. But the mockers of today will be destroyed as well.

Here is another question: But why would God destroy people whom He created? Here is the answer:

"Then the LORD saw that the wickedness of man was great in the earth, and that every intent of the thoughts of his heart was only evil continually. And the LORD was sorry that He had made man on the earth, and He was grieved in His heart. So the LORD said, "I will destroy man whom I have created from the face of the earth, both man and beast, creeping thing and birds of the air, for I am sorry that I have made them." (Genesis 6:5–7)

The people in Noah's day became so very wicked because all their thoughts were evil continually. The Lord Jesus Christ spoke of the future and final generation that would eerily resemble Noah's. So let's go back to Genesis—the only book and the only place where you can find where we came from, who we are, and why we are here.

"Now it came to pass, when men began to multiply on the face of the earth . . ." (Genesis 6:1a)

In Noah's day there was a great population explosion as men began to multiply on the face of the earth.

QUESTION: How many people do you think lived on planet earth in 1350?
ANSWER: 370,000,000 (370 million)[1]
QUESTION: How many in 1804?
ANSWER: 1,000,000,000 (1 billion)[2]—un.org
In 2012 there are 7,000,000,000 (7 billion) people on the planet earth[3]—sciencebase.com

Like Noah's day we are in a population explosion! What other characteristics, beyond incredible population increase, were the characteristics in Noah's day?

Sexual Impurity

As mentioned before evil thoughts and wicked behavior have caused a worldwide movement of homosexuality, including same sex marriage, which is sweeping the globe!

"Do you not know that the unrighteous will not inherit the kingdom of God? Do not be deceived. Neither fornicators, nor idolaters, nor adulterers, nor homosexuals, nor sodomites, nor thieves, nor covetous, nor drunkards, nor revilers, nor extortioners will inherit the kingdom of God." (1 Corinthians 6:9–10)

Fornication is any sex outside of Biblical marriage between a man and a woman. Our Lord Jesus tells us:

"But from the beginning of the creation, God 'made them male and female.' 'For this reason a man shall leave his father and mother and be joined to his wife, and the two shall become one flesh'; so then they are no longer two, but one flesh." (Mark 10:6–8)

Today, marriage is scoffed at and under attack as fornicators live together and men and women assert marriage within their gender. Rape, murder, sexual perversion, cross dressing, homosexuality, and pornography are all being accepted as normal like never before in our country! Every evil thing under the sun is called good and that which has traditionally been known as good is called evil:

"Woe to those who call evil good, and good evil; Who put darkness for light, and light for darkness; Who put bitter for sweet, and sweet for bitter!" (Isaiah 5:20)

Violence

"The earth also was corrupt before God, and the earth was filled with violence." (Genesis 6:11)

"And God said to Noah, "The end of all flesh has come before Me, for the earth is filled with violence through them; and behold, I will destroy them with the earth." (Genesis 6:13)

Here is a statistic that demonstrates how violent our society is today: globally approximately 44,000,000 (44 million) babies are killed annually in their mother's womb.[4] If you add those numbers annually back to 1980 the number of murdered babies doubles the deaths from all major wars and genocides in the last 2000 years COMBINED! This would include genocides like: Jewish Holocaust, Cambodia, Serbia, Rwanda, Congo . . . and these only date back to the last seventy-five years! This is the most violent generation in the history of the world—-much more than in Noah's day!

Remember, the Lord Jesus said speaking of Himself:

"And as it was in the days of Noah, so it will be also in the days of the Son of Man . . ." (Luke 17:26)

"For the Son of Man will come in the glory of His Father with His angels, and then He will reward each according to his works." (Matthew 16:27)

What does this mean? The Lord Jesus is coming very soon, and boy is He mad! What is the manner of His return?

. . . in flaming fire taking vengeance on those who do not know God, and on those who do not obey the gospel of our Lord Jesus Christ. These shall be punished with everlasting destruction from the presence of the Lord and from the glory of His power, when He comes, in that Day, to be glorified in His saints and to be admired among all those who believe, because our testimony among you was believed. (2 Thessalonians 2:8–10)

And for those mocking today, as the above verse mentions, they will not be destroyed by a flood, but by fire:

···· *knowing this first: that scoffers will come in the last days, walking according to their own lusts, and saying, "Where is the promise of His coming? For since the fathers fell asleep, all things continue as they were from the beginning of creation." For this they willfully forget: that by the word of God the heavens were of old, and the earth standing out of water and in the water, by which the world that then existed perished, being flooded with water. But the heavens and the earth which are now preserved by the same word, are reserved for fire until the day of judgment and perdition of ungodly men. (2 Peter 3:3–7)*

Dear friend, the mocking of the things God loves and the embracing of those things He hates is about to have a very tragic and abrupt end—the risen Lord Jesus is coming soon. Are you ready? If you will hear, believe, and obey the gospel (good news) of Jesus Christ you will be forgiven by God the Father and experience the love, kindness, goodness, and mercy of the Lord Jesus Christ! He doesn't want to punish you. Listen to what He said to Israel:

"Say to them: 'As I live,' says the Lord GOD, 'I have no pleasure in the death of the wicked, but that the wicked turn from his way and live. Turn, turn from your evil ways! For why should you die, O house of Israel?' (Ezekiel 33:11)

In the same way He wants you to turn (repent) from your evil ways and turn to the gospel of Jesus Christ and LIVE FOREVER with Him today and in Heaven in the next life. You may say, "I don't have any evil ways." Not believing in the gospel of Jesus Christ and thinking that you are good enough to go to heaven without Jesus Christ is evil. We have seen that in the scriptures above. But just in case that is not enough here is a Bible verse that makes it clear:

"But the cowardly, unbelieving, abominable, murderers, sexually immoral, sorcerers, idolaters, and all liars shall have their part in the lake which burns with fire and brimstone, which is the second death." (Revelation 21:8)

Have you ever been any of these things listed in Revelation 21:8? I know I have. But, as the author of this book I can tell you that I have been saved from my sin and will be with my Lord Jesus forever—He is in my heart and life! What must I do to be saved? Know that in spite of your sins God loves you very much. How much? This much:

> *"For God so loved the world that He gave His only begotten Son, that whoever believes in Him should not perish but have ever- lasting life." (John 3:16)*

God the Father loves you so much that He gave His only begotten Son Jesus Christ to die a horribly painful, humiliating, and unde- served death on the cross for your sins. He was buried and rose again on the third day! He is the sinless Son of God that gave His innocent life to pay for our guilt and sin. He has gone back to our Father in heaven and has placed His loving good news (the gospel) in your hands today so that you can be forgiven and saved from the punishment for your sins!

He will then place you in Christ and send His Holy Spirit to live in you to help you live a life that honors Father God. This is called being born again.

> *"Jesus answered and said to him, "Most assuredly, I say to you, unless one is born again, he cannot see the kingdom of God." (John 3:3)*

> *"Therefore, if anyone is in Christ, he is a new creation; old things have passed away; behold, all things have become new." (2 Cor- inthians 5:17)*

Will you believe in Him? Will you turn away from your sins? The greatest sin of all is unbelief. Will you seek to live a life that honors our Heavenly Father?

If so, begin that new life with this prayer: Holy Father in heaven, I have sinned against you and I do not want your punishment. I know that you love me enough that You sent the Savior Jesus Christ to die on the cross for my sins. I believe He rose from the grave on the third day. Father in Heaven please forgive me and give me a new life in Christ Jesus!

Now, together let's all make a beeline for *America's Ark.*

End Notes

Chapter 3:

1. Puritans Quote, http://www.massmoments.org/moment.cfm?mid=106.
2. Delaware Charter, Avalon Project Yale Law School. http://avalon.law.yale.edu/18th_century/de01.asp.
3. Constitution of Maryland, November 11, 1776, Avalon Project Yale Law School http://avalon.law.yale.edu/17th_century/ma02.asp.
4. List of Signers of the Constitution: Christian Background of Signers of the Constitution, http://churchvstate.blogspot.com/2007/10/our-founders-were-they-christian.html.
5. Quote from Declaration of Independence, http://www.ushistory.org/Declaration/document/.
6. George Washington's Speech to Delaware Indian Chiefs on May 12, 1779, in John C. Fitzpatrick, editor, *The Writings of George Washington*, Vol. XV (Washington: U.S. Government Printing Office, 1932), p. 55. http://www.christiananswers.net/q-wall/wal-g011.html.
7. Thomas Jefferson on God's wrath, John McTernan's Insights, http://defendproclaimthefaith.org/blog/?tag=obama-as-president.
8. James Madison to the General Assembly of the State of Virginia: John McTernan's Insights, http://defendproclaimthefaith.org/blog/?tag=obama-as-president.
9. *The Correspondence and Public Papers of John Jay*, Henry P. Johnston, ed., (New York: Burt Franklin, 1970), Vol. IV, p. 393. class-8commentary.blogspot.com/2006/10/.

10. *The Washington Monument: Hallowed Ground: Washington's Monuments to Faith, Family and Freedom,* by Chuck Donovan and Christina Darnell, religiousliberty.com/article-washington-dc-monuments.htm.
11. President Abraham Lincoln's Proclamation: A Day Of National Humiliation, Fasting, and Prayer in the United States Of America on April 30, 1863, www.quietwaters.org/abraham_lincoln_national_day_of_prayer.htm.

Chapter 4:

1. School Prayer In America: http://www.schoolprayerinamerica.info/.
2. National Park Service U.S. Department of the Interior- http://www.nps.gov/jeff/historyculture/upload/mcguffey.pdf.
3. The McGuffey Readers—1836 version, by Shannon Payne http://www.nd.edu/~rbarger/www7/mcguffey.html.
4. Noah Webster, http://www.faithofourfathers.net/webster.html.
5 www.answersingenesis.org/ . . . /harvard-yale-princeton . . . once-christian.
6. "The Greatness of America," Laurie Gregg, *CP Living*, May 25, 2009. http://www.christianpost.com/news/the-greatness-of-america-38788/ (*There is some dispute, in terms of its authenticity as it relates to De Tocqueville. Some question this commonly attributed quote as not originating from his *Democracy in America*.).
7. William J. Federer quotes Alexis de Tocqueville-Democracy In America from America's God and Country, http://www.ministers-best-friend.com/Alexis-de-Tocqueville-Quotes-on-Christian-America.html.

Chapter 5:

1. Charles Spurgeon quote, Hatikvah Film Trust, *The Cyrus Call*, produced and directed by Hugh Kitson, 2008.
2. Charles Wesley, Song from the Wesley's hymnal 1779, Hatikvah Film Trust, *The Cyrus Call*, produced and directed by Hugh Kitson, 2008.
3. Lord Palmerston quote: *The Cyrus Call*, produced and directed by Hugh Kitson, 2008.
4. The Balfour Declaration, November 2, 1917: Israel Ministry of Foreign Affairs, http://www.mfa.gov.il/MFA/Peace%20Process/

Guide%20to%20the%20Peace%20Process/The%20Balfour%20 Declaration.

5. *Jewish American Patriots*, John McTernan: As America Has Done To Israel, pgs 56, 64. 2006,2008.

6. An Example Of A Blessed Society: John McTernan: *As America Has Done To Israel* Pg 269. 2006,2008./ http://www.teachin- gamericanhistory.org/library/index.asp?document=397.

7. Signers of Blackstone Memorial, John McTernan: *As America Has Done To Israel* Pg 78,79. 2006,2008.

Chapter 6:

1. Presidents and Secret Societies: http://www.directoryupdate. net/presidents.html.

2. Madrid Peace Conference October 1991, Israel: the Blessing and the Curse. Pg 60,61. by John McTernan and Bill Koenig. 2001.

3. http://abcnews.go.com/Politics/story?id=193746&page=1#. UVXIiVcOYnR

4. Barack Obama quote, John McTernan's blog: http://www.defend- proclaimthefaith.org/blog/.

5 40 Percent Of Americans Still Believe In Creationism: Huffington Post/Gallup Poll November 2010 http://www.huffingtonpost. com/2010/12/20/40-of-americans-still-bel_n_799078.html.

6. A left-wing monopoly on campuses, by Jeff Jacoby of The Boston Globe, December 2, 2004 http://www.boston.com/news/globe/ editorial_opinion/oped/articles/2004/12/02/a_left_wing_ monopoly_on_campuses/.

7. Bibles out, gay pride in, by Chad Groening, June 20, 2012 http:// onenewsnow.com/culture/2012/06/20/bibles-nah-gay-pride- yep.

8. Corporations Urge Supreme Court to Embrace Gay Marriage, by Lawrence Hurley and Aruna Viswanatha, Reuters, February 27, 2013. http://www.reuters.com/assets/print?aid=USBRE91Q 0IG20130227.

9. First Ever Gay Pride Event at Pentagon Features Messages from President and Defense Secretary on Video, by Penny Starr, CNS news http://cnsnews.com/news/article/first-ever-gay-pride-event- pentagon-features-messages-president-and-defense-secretary/.

Chapter 8:

1. Midwest drought worsens, food inflation to rise, Wed, Jul 25 2012, By Peter Bohan and Russ Blinch, http://www.reuters.com/article/2012/07/25/usa-drought-idUSL2E8IPFHF20120725.

2. Brutal July heat a new U.S. record, CNN.com http://www.cnn.com/2012/08/08/us/temperature-record/index.html.

3. Drought's impact on food prices could worsen hunger in America, http://news.yahoo.com/blogs/lookout/drought-impact-food-prices-could-worsen-hunger-america-130019526.html.

4. Hummingbirds, facing drought and food shortage, get some human help, http://www.cbsnews.com/8301–18563_162–57494003/hummingbirds-facing-drought-and-food-shortage-get-some-human-help/?tag=nl.e875.

5. Cows eating candy during the drought, WPRI.com Eyewitness News, Thursday, 16 Aug 2012MAYFIELD http://www.wpri.com/dpps/entertainment/must_see_video/cows-eating-candy-during-the-drought-nd12-jgr_4323303.

6. Food shortages could force world into vegetarianism, warn scientists, The Guardian UK-8/28/2012, http://www.guardian.co.uk/global-development/2012/aug/26/food-shortages-world-vegetarianism.

7. Record-breaking wildfire season could get worse in Texas, By Ramit Plushnick-Masti and Christopher Sherman. The Associated Press, September 12, 2011. http://www.firerescue1.com/urban-interface/articles/1122081-Record-breaking-wildfire-season-could-get-worse-in-Texas/.

8. Record breaking heat as Colorado fires rage across the state, Examiner.com, June 24, 2012, by Dorsi Diaz, http://www.examiner.com/article/record-breaking-heat-as-colorado-fires-rage-across-the-state.

9. Wyoming Wildfire Grows As Montana And Colorado Fires Continue To Burn, by Kristen Wyatt, July 4, 2012 http://www.huffingtonpost.com/2012/07/04/wyoming-wildfire-colorado-wildfire_n_1649766.html.

Chapter 9:

1. Big Fishes Of The World, http://bigfishesoftheworld.blogspot.com/2012/02/shark-bull-carcharinus-leucas.html.

2. Surfer, swimmer, shark! Attacks on the rise, by Tim Friend, USA TODAY, July 24, 2001. http://usatoday30.usatoday.com/news/science/2001–07–25-shark-attacks.htm.
3. Shark attacks rise, fishing tactics may be at fault, by Michelle, Limited Lands August-6–2012, http://www.limitedlands.com/2012/08/06/shark-attacks-rise-fishing-tactics-maybe-at-fault/.
4. Shark Attack in Cape Cod, www.sportfishermen.com/board/f17/shark-attack-cape-cod-2457143.html *and* http://www.foxnews.com/us/2012/07/31/man-attacked-by-shark-off-popular-cape-cod-beach/, July 31, 2012.
5. Sharks Populations Decreasing, Attacks on the Rise—Science, http://www.redorbit.com/news/science/1624397/sharks_populations_decreasing_attacks_on_the_rise/.
6. Are Sharks More Likely to Attack in American Waters?, by Eli MacKinnon, Life's Little Mysteries Staff Writer, August 22 2012 http://www.livescience.com/22587-america-shark-attacks.html.
7. California surfer killed in shark attack CBS, Leah Thompson, CBS News. October 24, 2012. http://www.cbsnews.com/8301–501843_162–57538963/california-surfer-killed-in-shark-attack/.
8. Multiple sightings of great white sharks forces closure of Cape, Victoria Cavaliere, New York Daily News, September 1, 2012. http://www.nydailynews.com/news/national/multiple-sightings-great-white-sharks-forces-closure-cape-beach-article-1.1149562.
9. Great white sharks: Close encounters on East and West coasts: By Shanna McCord, Associated Press and Santa Cruz Sentinel, July 9, 2012. http://www.csmonitor.com/USA/Latest-News-Wires/2012/0709/Great-white-sharks-Close-encounters-on-East-and-West-coasts-video.
10. Black bears fight each other in front yard of Florida home, By Dave McDaniel, June 22, 2012. www.ksdk.com/news/article/325217/28/Black-bears-fight-each-other.
11. Fatal Black Bear Attacks on the Rise, http://news.discovery.com/animals/black-bear-attacks-north-america-110511.html.
12. Bear Attacks on the Rise in North and South Carolina, May 28, 2007. http://voices.yahoo.com/bear-attacks-rise-north-south-carolina-364414.html.
13. Bear Attacks in Central New Hampshire on the Rise, Yahoo! http://voices.yahoo.com/bear-attacks-central-hampshire-rise-1539295.html?cat=8.

14. Deadly Bear Attacks Could Rise - ABC News, Aug 27, 2010. http://abcnews.go.com/Nightline/deadly-bear-attacks-rise/story?id=11499044#.UO2tuaVTtSU.

15. Are Hungry Bears in Yellowstone Attacking Humans for Food? By Jeff Hull, Outside Magazine, June 2012. http://www.outsideonline.com/outdoor-adventure/natural-intelligence/the-grizzly-truth.html.

16. Coyote Attacks on the rise in Los Angeles: Meeting September 5, by Becky Starr, examiner.com, August 29, 2012. http://www.examiner.com/article/coyote-attacks-on-the-rise-los-angeles-meeting-september-5–2012.

17. On the Loose: Urban Coyotes Thrive in North American Cities, Research News 1/3/2005 http://researchnews.osu.edu/archive/urbcoyot.htm.

18. Animal Attacks Against Man on the Rise, ABCNews.com, Feb 16, 2011. http://abcnews.go.com/Nightline/video/man-beast-12937549.

19. Cougar Attacks Increasing in West, The Associated Press http://www.igorilla.com/gorilla/animal/cougar_attacks_increasing.html.

20. Wild boars invade New York State; kill pets, chase people, by Ray Sanchez, Reuters, July 29, 2011. http://www.reuters.com/article/2011/07/29/us-wildboar-newyork-idUSTRE76S3I220110729.

21. Frustrated Residents: Raccoons Slowly Taking Over New York City, CBS New York, October 5, 2012. http://newyork.cbslocal.com/2012/10/05/frustrated-residents-raccoons-slowly-taking-over-new-york-city/.

22. Bedbugs an increasing concern at DNC hotel, by David Hill, The Washington Times, September 3, 2012. http://www.washingtontimes.com/news/2012/sep/3/bedbugs-an-increasing-concern-at-dnc-hotels/.

23. Mutated pests are quickly adapting to biotech crops in unpredicted and disturbing ways, by John McTernan, July 2, 2012. http://defendproclaimthefaith.org/blog/?tag=landers-earthquake.

24. Can Pesticides Cause ADHD?, by Andrea Canning and Jennifer Pereira, ABC News, May 17, 2010. http://abcnews.go.com/GMA/OnCall/pesticides-contribute-attention-deficit-hyperactivity-disorder/story?id=10662790#.UO26BKVTtSU.

Chapter 10:

1. Mega church pastor beaten to death with electric guitar by man who rammed car into church, by Peter Rugg, Mail Online, October 29, 2012. http://www.dailymail.co.uk/news/article-2225061/ Church-pastor-killed-Rev-Danny-Kirk-Sr-beaten-death-electric-guitar.html#ixzz2AoSqPkKV.
2. Enter At Your Own Risk: Police Union Says 'War-Like' Detroit Is Unsafe For Visitors, Local CBS Detroit, October 6, 2012. http://detroit.cbslocal.com/2012/10/06/enter-at-your-own-risk-police-union-says-war-like-detroit-is-unsafe-for-visitors/.
3. Chicago police confirm 'tragic number' of 500 homicides, by Jeremy Gorner and Peter Nickeas Chicago Tribune, December 28, 2012. http://articles.chicagotribune.com/2012–12–28/news/chi-chicago-2012-homicide-toll-20121228_1_latest-homicide-500th-homicide-tragic-number.
4. Queens father fatally crushed by train, By Kirstan Conley, Larry Celona, Antonio Antenucci, Christina Carrega and Jeane MacIntosh, New York Post, December 5, 2012. http://www.nypost.com/p/news/local/manhattan/nightmare_on_subway_tracks_GgvCtkeJj6cTeyxHns2VNP.
5. Execution Style Slayings Leave 4 Dead In Detroit, Local CBS Detroit, December 5, 2012. http://detroit.cbslocal.com/2012/12/05/no-arrests-in-deaths-of-4-killed-execution-style/
6. Suspect Attacked, Robbed 85-Year-Old Woman In Elevator, CBS New York, December 10, 2012. http://newyork.cbslocal.com/2012/12/10/nypd-suspect-attacked-robbed-85-year-old-woman-in-elevator/.
7. Man brutally shot in head in broad daylight, by Kirstan Conley and Larry Celona, New York Post, December 10, 2012. http://www.nypost.com/p/news/local/manhattan/man_shot_in_head_in_broad_daylight_5lOmcRkgAkYeO3flFNuXxO.
8. Man and woman found bound and gagged on San Francisco street, By NBC News staff, NBC News.com, December 10, 2012. http://usnews.nbcnews.com/_news/2012/12/10/15821784-man-and-woman-found-bound-and-gagged-on-san-francisco-street.
9. Clackamas Town Center shooting, December 11, 2012. http://www.oregonlive.com/clackamascounty/index.ssf/2012/12/clackamas_town_center_shooting.html.

10. Mother killed right outside Brookdale Hospital, where she was visiting sick daughter, New York Post, Jessica Simeone, Reuven Fenton and Dan Mangan, December 12, 2012. http://www.nypost.com/p/news/local/brooklyn/slain_right_tside_hosp_dHmFEnGIripwOwOH5TCCvN.
11. Multiple Deaths, Including Children, At Sandy Hook School Shooting In Newtown, TIME Newsfeed, December 14, 2012. http://newsfeed.time.com/2012/12/14/school-shooting-reported-in-newtown-conn/.
12. Taliban mock US as Afghan war enters 12th year, October 7, 2012. http://www.freerepublic.com/focus/f-news/2941565/posts.
13. 'Queen James Bible': Now There's a Gay-Friendly Version of Scripture, by John McTernan, December 23, 2012. http://defend-proclaimthefaith.org/blog/?p=3380.

Chapter 11:

1. Dallas mayor declares emergency over West Nile virus, Reuters, by Marice Richter, August 15, 2012. http://www.reuters.com/article/2012/08/15/us-usa-health-westnile-idUS-BRE87E0ZO20120815.
2. Dallas launches aerial defense to fight West Nile virus, Fox News.com, August 17, 2012. http://www.foxnews.com/us/2012/08/17/dallas-launches-aerial-defense-to-fight-west-nile-virus/?test=latestnews.
3. West Nile outbreak largest ever in U.S., by Elizabeth Cohen, CNN.com, August 22, 2012. http://www.cnn.com/2012/08/22/health/west-nile-virus/index.html.
4. Manhattan to be sprayed against West Nile virus, Medical Express, August 28, 2012. http://medicalxpress.com/news/2012–08-manhattan-west-nile-virus.html.
5. CDC: More than 1,100 cases of West Nile reported through August, by Elizabeth Prann, Fox News.com, August 22, 2012. http://www.foxnews.com/health/2012/08/22/cdc-alarming-increase-seen-in-west-nile-cases/.
6. West Nile virus cases rise 40 percent in one week, myfoxny.com, August 29, 2012. http://www.myfoxny.com/story/19408039/west-nile-virus-cases-rise-40-percent-in-week.
7. West Nile Virus Cases Set Record, Deaths Soar, Huffpost, August 29, 2012. http://www.huffingtonpost.com/2012/08/29/west-nile-virus-cases-deaths_n_1840117.html.

8. NIH superbug claims 7th victim, Brian Vastag and Lena H. Sun, The Washington Post, September 14, 2012. http://www.washingtonpost.com/national/health-science/nih-superbug-claims-7th-victim/2012/09/14/09b3742e-fe9b-11e1-b153–218509a954e1_story.html.
9. Second person dies after contracting rare rodent-borne disease at Yosemite, FoxNews.com, August 28, 2012. http://www.foxnews.com/health/2012/08/28/second-person-dies-after-contracting-rare-rodent-borne-disease-at-yosemite/#ixzz24ofIeMHz.
10. CDC says 10,000 at risk of hantavirus in Yosemite outbreak, by Dan Whitcomb and Ronnie Cohen, Reuters, August 31, 2012. http://www.reuters.com/article/2012/08/31/us-usa-hantavirus-yosemite-idUSBRE87U04P20120831.
11. Third Yosemite visitor dies of hantavirus; eight now infected, Los Angeles Times, September 6, 2012. http://latimesblogs.latimes.com/lanow/2012/09/yosemite-hantavirus-third-death.html.
12. Colorado girl recovering from bubonic plague, FoxNews.com, September 6, 2012. http://www.foxnews.com/health/2012/09/05/colorado-girl-recovering-from-bubonic-plague/?test=latestnews.
13. Frustrated UWS Resident Hangs "Rat Crossing" Signs NBC News, by Andrew Mach, NBCNews.com, August 30, 2012. http://usnews.nbcnews.com/_news/2012/08/30/13570221-fed-up-with-rodent-infestation-new-york-man-hangs-rat-crossing-signs?lite.
14. AIDS epidemic in Washington, DC Public Radio International, January 6, 2010. http://www.pri.org/stories/health/aids-epidemic-in-washington-dc1819.html.
15. African monkey meat that could be behind the next HIV—Health News—Health & Families, by Evan Williams, The Independent, May 25, 2012. http://www.independent.co.uk/life-style/health-and-families/health-news/african-monkey-meat-that-could-be-behind-the-next-hiv-7786152.html.
16. Chagas Disease, an incurable infection, called the 'new AIDS of the Americas,' by Meghan Neal, NY Daily News, May 29, 2012. http://www.nydailynews.com/life-style/health/incurable-infection-called-new-aids-americas-report-article-1.1086053#ixzz2GkMT3m8M.
17. Woman pastor DIES after contracting flesh-eating bug in SIXTH case of deadly bacteria identified in America, by Phil Vinter,

Mail Online, June 14, 2012. http://www.dailymail.co.uk/news/article-2159123/Deadly-flesh-eating-bacteria-claims-life-sixth-case-killer-infection-identified.html.

18. Drug-Resistant Gonorrhea: Is The Antibiotic Era Coming To An End?, By Cara Santa Maria, October 11, 2012. http://www.huffingtonpost.com/2012/10/11/antibiotic-resistance-gonorrhea_n_1916862.html#slide=402321.

19. Dengue re-emerges in Florida, by Robert Preidt, USA Today, July 16, 2010. http://usatoday30.usatoday.com/news/health/2010–07–15-dengue-fever_N.htm.

20. Dengue fever confirmed in Florida girl, USA Today, September 27, 2012. http://usatoday30.usatoday.com/news/nation/story/2012/09/27/dengue-fever-confirmed-in-florida-girl/57848484/1.

21. 2 die in Legionnaires' outbreak linked to Chicago hotel, By Mitch Smith chicagotribune.com, August 28, 2012. http://articles.chicagotribune.com/2012–08–28/news/ct-met-legionnaires-disease-marriott-20120828_1_legionella-bacteria-legionnaires-outbreak.

22. Study Links Cat Litter Box to Increased Suicide Risk, By Susan Donaldson James, ABC News, July 2, 2012. http://abcnews.go.com/Health/litter-box-parasite-toxoplasma-linked-higher-suicide-risk/story?id=16698365.

23. Flea-Borne Typhus Reported On The Rise In Orange County CBS Los Angeles, September 14, 2011. http://losangeles.cbslocal.com/2011/09/14/flea-borne-typhus-reported-on-the-rise-in-orange-county/.

24. Woman Who Contracted Bacterial Infection Caused By Dog's Saliva Dies, CBS Atlanta, September 5, 2012. http://atlanta.cbslocal.com/2012/09/05/woman-with-flesh-eating-illness-dies/.

25. New Species Of Ticks Spreading Disease Across Southeast, CBS Charlotte, May 28, 2012. http://charlotte.cbslocal.com/2012/05/28/new-species-of-ticks-spreading-disease-across-southeast/.

26. Toxic green slime has taken over the lakes of America. Again. By John Upton, September 17, 2012. http://grist.org/food/toxic-green-slime-has-taken-over-the-lakes-of-america-again/.

Chapter 12:

1. *Theological Wordbook Of The Old Testament* pg 752 Laird Harris, Gleason Archer, Bruce Waltke. 2003.

Chapter 18:

1. 370 Million people on the earth, http://www.mashpedia.com/world_population.
2. 1 Billion people on the earth. http://www.un.org/esa/population/publications/sixbillion/sixbilpart1.pdf.
3. 7 Billion people on the earth, by David Bradley, Science Base, October 31, 2011. http://www.sciencebase.com/science-blog/world-population-reaches-7-billion-today-or-next-april.html.
4. Dr. Michael Brown, The Voice of Revolution, www.voiceofrevolution.com/2009/01/18/abortion-statistics.

Bibliography

40 Percent Of Americans Still Believe In Creationism: Huffington Post/ Gallup Poll November 2010. http://www.huffingtonpost. com/2010/12/20/40-of-americans-still-bel_n_799078.html

1 Billion people on the earth. http://www.un.org/esa/population/ publications/sixbillion/sixbilpart1.pdf

370 Million people on the earth, http://www.mashpedia.com/ world_population

AIDS epidemic in Washington, DC Public Radio International, January 6, 2010. http://www.pri.org/stories/health/aids-epidemic-in-washington-dc1819.html

Animal Attacks Against Man on the Rise, ABCNews.com, Feb 16, 2011. http://abcnews.go.com/Nightline/video/man-beast-12937549

Bear Attacks in Central New Hampshire on the Rise, Yahoo! http://voices.yahoo.com/bear-attacks-central-hampshire-rise-1539295.html?cat=8

Bear Attacks on the Rise in North and South Carolina, May 28, 2007. http://voices.yahoo.com/bear-attacks-rise-north-south-carolina-364414.html

Big Fishes Of The World, http://bigfishesoftheworld.blogspot. com/2012/02/shark-bull-carcharinus-leucas.html

Bohan, Peter and Russ Blinch, Midwest drought worsens, food inflation to rise, Wed, Jul 25 2012. http://www.reuters.com/ article/2012/07/25/usa-drought-idUSL2E8IPFHF20120725

Bradley, David. 7 Billion people on the earth, Science Base, October 31, 2011. http://www.sciencebase.com/science-blog/world-population-reaches-7-billion-today-or-next-april.html

Brutal July heat a new U.S. record, CNN.com http://www.cnn. com/2012/08/08/us/temperature-record/index.html

Bush on Religion and God, abcNews October 26, 2004. http://abcnews. go.com/Politics/story?id=193746&page=1#.UVXI-lc0YnR

Canning, Andrea and Jennifer Pereira. Can Pesticides Cause ADHD?, ABC News, May 17, 2010. http://abcnews.go.com/GMA/ OnCall/pesticides-contribute-attention-deficit-hyperactivity-disorder/story?id=10662790#.UO26BKVTtSU

Cavaliere, Victoria. Multiple sightings of great white sharks forces closure of Cape, New York Daily News, September 1, 2012. http://www.nydailynews.com/news/national/multiple-sightings-great-white-sharks-forces-closure-cape-beach-article-1.1149562

Christian Background of Signers of the Constitution, October 25, 2007. http://churchvstate.blogspot.com/2007/10/our-founders-were-they-christian.html

Clackamas Town Center shooting, December 11, 2012. http://www. oregonlive.com/clackamascounty/index.ssf/2012/12/clack-amas_town_center_shooting.html

Cohen, Elizabeth. West Nile outbreak largest ever in U.S., CNN.com, August 22, 2012. http://www.cnn.com/2012/08/22/health/west-nile-virus/index.html

Colorado girl recovering from bubonic plague, FoxNews.com, September 6, 2012. http://www.foxnews.com/health/2012/09/05/colorado-girl-recovering-from-bubonic-plague/?test=latestnews

Conley, Kirstan and Larry Celona. Man brutally shot in head in broad daylight, New York Post, December 10, 2012. http://www.nypost.com/p/news/local/manhattan/man_shot_in_head_in_broad_daylight_5lOmcRkgAkYeO3fIFNuXxO

Conley, Kirstan, Larry Celona, Antonio Antenucci, Christina Carrega and Jeane MacIntosh. Queens father fatally crushed by train, New York Post, December 5, 2012. http://www.nypost.com/p/news/local/manhattan/nightmare_on_subway_tracks_GgvCtkeJj6cTeyxHns2VNP

Constitution of Maryland, November 11, 1776, Avalon Project Yale Law School. http://avalon.law.yale.edu/17th_century/ma02.asp

Cougar Attacks Increasing in West, The Associated Press http://www.igorilla.com/gorilla/animal/cougar_attacks_increasing.html

Cows eating candy during the drought, WPRI.com Eyewitness News, Thursday, August 16, 2012. http://www.wpri.com/dpps/entertainment/must_see_video/cows-eating-candy-during-the-drought-nd12-jgr_4323303

Dallas launches aerial defense to fight West Nile virus, Fox News.com, August 17, 2012. http://www.foxnews.com/us/2012/08/17/dallas-launches-aerial-defense-to-fight-west-nile-virus/?test=latestnews

Declaration of Independence, http://www.ushistory.org/Declaration/document/

Delaware Charter, Avalon Project Yale Law School http://avalon.law.yale.edu/18th_century/de01.asp

Dengue fever confirmed in Florida girl, USA Today, September 27, 2012. http://usatoday30.usatoday.com/news/nation/story/2012/09/27/dengue-fever-confirmed-in-florida-girl/57848484/1

Diaz, Dorsi. Record breaking heat as Colorado fires rage across the state, Examiner.com, June 24, 2012, http://www.examiner.com/article/record-breaking-heat-as-colorado-fires-rage-across-the-state

Doane, Seth. Hummingbirds, facing drought and food shortage, get some human help, August 16, 2012. http://www.cbsnews.com/8301–18563_162–57494003/humming-birds-facing-drought-and-food-shortage-get-some-human-help/?tag=nl.e875

Donovan, Chuck and Christina Darnell., The Washington Monument: Hallowed Ground: Washington's Monuments to Faith, Family and Freedom, http://religiousliberty.com/index.htm

Dr. Brown, Michael The Voice of Revolution, www.voiceofrevolution.com/2009/01/18/abortion-statistics

Enter At Your Own Risk: Police Union Says 'War-Like' Detroit Is Unsafe For Visitors, Local CBS Detroit, October 6, 2012. http://detroit.cbslocal.com/2012/10/06/enter-at-your-own-risk-police-union-says-war-like-detroit-is-unsafe-for-visitors/

Execution Style Slayings Leave 4 Dead In Detroit, Local CBS Detroit, December 5, 2012. http://detroit.cbslocal.com/2012/12/05/ no-arrests-in-deaths-of-4-killed-execution-style/

Fatal Black Bear Attacks on the Rise, http://news.discovery.com/ animals/black-bear-attacks-north-america-110511.html

Federer, William J., Alexis de Tocqueville-Democracy In America from America's God and Country, http://www.ministers- best-friend.com/Alexis-de-Tocqueville-Quotes-on-Chris- tian-America.html

Flea-Borne Typhus Reported On The Rise In Orange County, CBS Los Angeles, September 14, 2011. http://losangeles.cbslocal. com/2011/09/14/flea-borne-typhus-reported-on-the-rise- in-orange-county/

Friend, Tim. Surfer, swimmer, shark! Attacks on the rise, USA TODAY, July 24, 2001. http://usatoday30.usatoday.com/news/science/ 2001–07–25-shark-attacks.htm

Frustrated Residents: Raccoons Slowly Taking Over New York City, CBS New York, October 5, 2012. http://newyork.cbslocal. com/2012/10/05/frustrated-residents-raccoons-slowly- taking-over-new-york-city/

George Washington's Speech to Delaware Indian Chiefs on May 12, 1779, in John C. Fitzpatrick, editor, The Writings of George Washington, Vol. XV (Washington: U.S. Government Printing Office, 1932), p. 55. http://www.christiananswers.net/q- wall/wal-g011.html

Gorner, Jeremy and Peter Nickeas. Chicago police confirm 'tragic number' of 500 homicides, Chicago Tribune, December 28, 2012. http://articles.chicagotribune.com/2012–12–28/ news/chi-chicago-2012-homicide-toll-20121228_1_latest- homicide-500th-homicide-tragic-number

Gregg, Laurie. The Greatness of America, CP Living, May 25, 2009. http://www.christianpost.com/news/the-greatness-of-america-38788/

Groening, Chad. Bibles out, gay pride in, June 20, 2012. http://one-newsnow.com/culture/2012/06/20/bibles-nah-gay-pride-yep

Harris, Laird, Gleason Archer and Bruce Waltke. Theological Wordbook Of The Old Testament pg 752. 2003

Hatikvah Film Trust, The Cyrus Call, produced and directed by Hugh Kitson, 2008

Hill, David. Bedbugs an increasing concern at DNC hotel, The Washington Times, September 3, 2012. http://www.washingtontimes.com/news/2012/sep/3/bedbugs-an-increasing-concern-at-dnc-hotels/

Hull, Jeff. Are Hungry Bears in Yellowstone Attacking Humans for Food?, Outside Magazine, June 2012. http://www.outside-online.com/outdoor-adventure/natural-intelligence/the-grizzly-truth.html

Hurley, Lawrence and Aruna Viswanatha. Corporations Urge Supreme Court to Embrace Gay Marriage, Reuters, February 27, 2013. http://www.reuters.com/assets/print?aid=USBRE91Q0IG20130227

Israel Ministry of Foreign Affairs, The Balfour Declaration, November 2, 1917. http://www.mfa.gov.il/MFA/Peace%20Process/Guide%20to%20the%20Peace%20Process/The%20Balfour%20Declaration

Jacoby, Jeff. A left-wing monopoly on campuses, The Boston Globe, December 2, 2004 http://www.boston.com/news/globe/editorial_opinion/oped/articles/2004/12/02/a_left_wing_monopoly_on_campuses/

James, Susan D. Study Links Cat Litter Box to Increased Suicide Risk, ABC News, July 2, 2012. http://abcnews.go.com/Health/litter-box-parasite-toxoplasma-linked-higher-suicide-risk/story?id=16698365

Johnston, Henry P., The Correspondence and Public Papers of John Jay, ed., (New York: Burt Franklin, 1970), Vol. IV, p. 393. class8commentary.blogspot.com/2006/10/

Lord Palmerston, The Cyrus Call, produced and directed by Hugh Kitson, 2008

Mach, Andrew. Frustrated UWS Resident Hangs "Rat Crossing" Signs NBC News, NBCNews.com, August 30, 2012. http://usnews.nbcnews.com/_news/2012/08/30/13570221-fed-up-with-rodent-infestation-new-york-man-hangs-rat-crossing-signs?lite

MacKinnon, Eli. Are Sharks More Likely to Attack in American Waters?, August 22 2012 http://www.livescience.com/22587-america-shark-attacks.html

Man and woman found bound and gagged on San Francisco street, NBC News.com, December 10, 2012. http://usnews.nbcnews.com/_news/2012/12/10/15821784-man-and-woman-found-bound-and-gagged-on-san-francisco-street

Manhattan to be sprayed against West Nile virus, Medical Express, August 28, 2012. http://medicalxpress.com/news/2012–08-manhattan-west-nile-virus.html

McCord, Shannon, Associated Press and Santa Cruz Sentinel. Great white sharks: Close encounters on East and West coasts, July 9, 2012. http://www.csmonitor.com/USA/Latest-News-Wires/2012/0709/Great-white-sharks-Close-encounters-on-East-and-West-coasts-video

McDaniel, Dave. Black bears fight each other in front yard of Florida home, June 22, 2012. www.ksdk.com/news/article/325217/28/Black-bears-fight-each-other

McTernan John., As America Has Done To Israel, pgs 56, 64, 2006,2008

McTernan, John and Bill Koenig., Israel: the Blessing and the Curse. Pg 60,61. 2001.

McTernan, John. 'Queen James Bible': Now There's a Gay-Friendly Version of Scripture, December 23, 2012. http://defendproclaimthefaith.org/blog/?p=3380

McTernan, John. http://www.defendproclaimthefaith.org/blog/

McTernan, John. Thomas Jefferson on God's wrath, John McTernan's Insights, http://defendproclaimthefaith.org/blog/?tag=landers-earthquake

McTernan, John., As America Has Done To Israel Pg 269, 2006,2008, http://www.teachingamericanhistory.org/library/index.asp?document=397

McTernan, John., As America Has Done To Israel Pg 78,79, 2006,2008

McTernan, John., James Madison to the General Assembly of the State of Virginia: John McTernan's Insights, http://defendproclaimthefaith.org/blog/?tag=obama-as-president

Multiple Deaths, Including Children, At Sandy Hook School Shooting In Newtown, TIME Newsfeed, December 14, 2012. http://newsfeed.time.com/2012/12/14/school-shooting-reported-in-newtown-conn/

National Park Service U.S. Department of the Interior http://www.nps.gov/jeff/historyculture/upload/mcguffey.pdf

Neal, Meghan. Chagas Disease, an incurable infection, called the 'new AIDS of the Americas,' NY Daily News, May 29, 2012. http://www.nydailynews.com/life-style/health/incur-able-infection-called-new-aids-americas-report-article-1.1086053#ixzz2GkMT3m8M

New Species Of Ticks Spreading Disease Across Southeast, CBS Charlotte, May 28, 2012. http://charlotte.cbslocal.com/2012/05/28/new-species-of-ticks-spreading-disease-across-southeast/

Noah Webster, http://www.faithofourfathers.net/webster.html

Payne, Shannon., The McGuffey Readers—1836 version, http://www.nd.edu/~rbarger/www7/mcguffey.html

Plushnick-Masti, Ramit and Christopher Sherman. Record-breaking wildfire season could get worse in Texas, The Associated Press, September 12, 2011. http://www.firerescue1.com/urban-interface/articles/1122081-Record-breaking-wild-fire-season-could-get-worse-in-Texas/

Prann, Elizabeth. CDC: More than 1,100 cases of West Nile reported through August, Fox News.com, August 22, 2012. http://www.foxnews.com/health/2012/08/22/cdc-alarming-increase-seen-in-west-nile-cases/

Preidt, Robert. Dengue re-emerges in Florida, USA Today, July 16, 2010. http://usatoday30.usatoday.com/news/health/2010—07—15-dengue-fever_N.htm

President Abraham Lincoln's Proclamation: A Day Of National Humil-iation, Fasting, and Prayer in the United States of America on April 30, 1863, www.quietwaters.org/abraham_lincoln_national_day_of_prayer.htm

Presidents and Secret Societies: http://www.directoryupdate.net/presidents.html

Puritans Quote, http://www.massmoments.org/moment.cfm?mid=106

Richter, Marice. Dallas mayor declares emergency over West Nile virus, Reuters, August 15, 2012. http://www.reuters.com/article/2012/08/15/us-usa-health-westnile-idUS-BRE87E0ZO20120815

Rooney, Brian and Melia Patria, Deadly Bear Attacks Could Rise ABC News, August 27, 2010. http://abcnews.go.com/Night-line/deadly-bear-attacks-rise/story?id=11499044#.UO2tu-aVTtSU

Rugg, Peter. Mega church pastor beaten to death with electric guitar by man who rammed car into church, Mail Online, October 29, 2012. http://www.dailymail.co.uk/news/article-2225061/Church-pastor-killed-Rev-Danny-Kirk-Sr-beaten-death-electric-guitar.html#ixzz2AoSqPkKV

Sanchez, Ray. Wild boars invade New York State; kill pets, chase people, Reuters, July 29, 2011. http://www.reuters.com/article/2011/07/29/us-wildboar-newyork-idUS-TRE76S3I220110729

Santa Maria, Cara. Drug-Resistant Gonorrhea: Is The Antibiotic Era Coming To An End?, October 11, 2012. http://www.huffingtonpost.com/2012/10/11/antibiotic-resistance-gonorrhea_n_1916862.html#slide=402321

School Prayer In America: http://www.schoolprayerinamerica.info/

Second person dies after contracting rare rodent-borne disease at Yosemite, FoxNews.com, August 28, 2012. http://www.foxnews.com/health/2012/08/28/second-person-dies-after-contracting-rare-rodent-borne-disease-at-yosemite/#ixzz24ofleMHz

Shark Attack in Cape Cod, www.sportfishermen.com/board/f17/shark-attack-cape-cod-2457143.html and http://www.foxnews.com/us/2012/07/31/man-attacked-by-shark-off-popular-cape-cod-beach/, July 31, 2012

Shark attacks rise, fishing tactics may be at fault, by Michelle, Limited Lands August-6–2012, http://www.limitedlands.com/2012/08/06/shark-attacks-rise-fishing-tactics-maybe-at-fault/

Sharks Populations Decreasing, Attacks on the Rise—Science, http://www.redorbit.com/news/science/1624397/sharks_populations_decreasing_attacks_on_the_rise/

Sickles, Jason. Drought's impact on food prices could worsen hunger in America, August 21, 2012. http://news.yahoo.com/blogs/lookout/drought-impact-food-prices-could-worsen-hunger-america-130019526.html

Simeone, Jessica, Reuven Fenton and Dan Mangan. Mother killed right outside Brookdale Hospital, where she was visiting sick daughter, New York Post, December 12, 2012. http://www.nypost.com/p/news/local/brooklyn/slain_right_tside_hosp_dHmFEnGIripwOw0H5TCCvN

Smith, Mitch. 2 die in Legionnaires' outbreak linked to Chicago hotel, chicagotribune.com, August 28, 2012. http://articles.chicagotribune.com/2012–08–28/news/ct-met-legion-naires-disease-marriott-20120828_1_legionella-bacteria-legionnaires-outbreak

Starr, Becky. Coyote Attacks on the rise in Los Angeles: Meeting September 5, examiner.com, August 29, 2012. http://

www.examiner.com/article/coyote-attacks-on-the-rise-los-angeles-meeting-september-5–2012

Starr, Penny. First Ever Gay Pride Event at Pentagon Features Messages from President and Defense Secretary on Video: CNS news http://cnsnews.com/news/article/first-ever-gay-pride-event-pentagon-features-messages-president-and-defense-secretary/

Suspect Attacked, Robbed 85-Year-Old Woman In Elevator, CBS New York, December 10, 2012. http://newyork.cbslocal.com/2012/12/10/nypd-suspect-attacked-robbed-85-year-old-woman-in-elevator/

Taliban mock US as Afghan war enters 12th year, October 7, 2012. http://www.freerepublic.com/focus/f-news/2941565/posts

Third Yosemite visitor dies of Hantavirus; eight now infected, Los Angeles Times, September 6, 2012. http://latimesblogs.latimes.com/lanow/2012/09/yosemite-hantavirus-third-death.html

Thompson, Leah. California surfer killed in shark attack, CBS News. October 24, 2012. http://www.cbsnews.com/8301–501843_162–57538963/california-surfer-killed-in-shark-attack/

Upton. John. Toxic green slime has taken over the lakes of America. Again., September 17, 2012. http://grist.org/food/toxic-green-slime-has-taken-over-the-lakes-of-america-again/

Vastag, Brian and Lena H. Sun. NIH superbug claims 7th victim, The Washington Post, September 14, 2012. http://www.washingtonpost.com/national/health-science/nih-superbug-claims-7th-victim/2012/09/14/09b3742e-fe9b-11e1-b153–218509a954e1_story.html

Vidal, John. Food shortages could force world into vegetarianism, warn scientists, The Guardian, August 26, 2012. http://www.guardian.co.uk/global-development/2012/aug/26/food-shortages-world-vegetarianism

Vinter, Phil. Woman pastor DIES after contracting flesh-eating bug in SIXTH case of deadly bacteria identified in America, Mail Online, June 14, 2012. http://www.dailymail.co.uk/news/article-2159123/Deadly-flesh-eating-bacteria-claims-life-sixth-case-killer-infection-identified.html

Wagner, Holly. On the Loose: Urban Coyotes Thrive in North American Cities, Research News January 3, 2005. http://research-news.osu.edu/archive/urbcoyot.htm

Wesley, Charles Song from the Wesley's hymnal 1779, Hatikvah Film Trust, The Cyrus Call, produced and directed by Hugh Kitson, 2008

West Nile virus cases rise 40 percent in one week, myfoxny.com, August 29, 2012. http://www.myfoxny.com/story/19408039/west-nile-virus-cases-rise-40-percent-in-week

West Nile Virus Cases Set Record, Deaths Soar, Huffpost, August 29, 2012. http://www.huffingtonpost.com/2012/08/29/west-nile-virus-cases-deaths_n_1840117.html

Whitcomb, Dan and Ronnie Cohen. CDC says 10,000 at risk of hantavirus in Yosemite outbreak, Reuters, August 31, 2012. http://www.reuters.com/article/2012/08/31/us-usa-hanta-virus-yosemite-idUSBRE87U04P20120831

Williams, Evan. African monkey meat that could be behind the next HIV—Health News—Health & Families, The Independent, May 25, 2012. http://www.independent.co.uk/life-style/

health-and-families/health-news/african-monkey-meat-
that-could-be-behind-the-next-hiv-7786152.html

Woman Who Contracted Bacterial Infection Caused By Dog's
Saliva Dies, CBS Atlanta, September 5, 2012. http://atlanta.
cbslocal.com/2012/09/05/woman-with-flesh-eating-ill-
ness-dies/

www.answersingenesis.org/ . . . /harvard-yale-princeton . . . once-
christian

Wyatt, Kristen. Wyoming Wildfire Grows As Montana And Colorado Fires Continue To Burn, July 4, 2012. http://www.
huffingtonpost.com/2012/07/04/wyoming-wildfire-colo-
rado-wildfire_n_1649766.html